Inside the Head of a "Bad" Kid:

An Autoethnography of Adversity to Resilience

Inside the Head of a "Bad" Kid:

An Autoethnography of Adversity to Resilience

Bonnie Laabs

INSIDE THE HEAD OF A "BAD" KID: AN AUTOEHTNOGRAPHY OF
ADVERSITY TO RESILIENCE © 2018 by Bonnie Laabs
All Rights Reserved.

Cover Design by Jason Biwer, Power Play Productions
Author Photo by Amy Rondeau Photography

ISBN-13: 978-0692168448
ISBN-10: 0692168443

I dedicate this work:

To the students who face a world of hurt
and try to learn anyway.

To my former teachers, and mentors who loved me
unconditionally.

In loving memory of Jane Larson.

Acknowledgements

Thank you Tim, Jerry, Rob, and Bhaskar. Your words of wisdom, insight and guidance throughout this process were greatly valued. Thank you for encouraging me to see my work through many lenses.

Thank you, Jerry, for your time, support, and guidance throughout my entire graduate program. I feel extremely fortunate to have had an advisor that believes in me as you do.

Thank you, Emily, for your extensive encouragement, advice, handholding, sushi sharing, and editing (;?) expertise. I would not have finished if not for your help!

Thank you, Kirsten, for being the most positive and encouraging person I know! You are the greatest defensive partner, on the ice and off.

Thank you to my fellow graduates, friends, and FYC cohort who encouraged and inspired me along the way: Emily, Rayane, Joe, Keri, Patti, Chris, Siri, Jolene, Chun, Young-Hoon, Colleen, and Sara.

Thank you Kyna for your never-ending support! You always know how to make me smile!

Thank you to my family who has grown with me, allowed me to share my story, and encouraged me along the way: Mom, Dad, Bruce, and extended family.

Thank you to my many friends, colleagues, and students who were part of my journey. Thank you for your enthusiasm, encouragement, and trust: Tyrone for giving me permission to implement the behavior intervention, Megan, for following the program, Steve, our conversations were invaluable, Bobbie your enthusiasm for my work, River Hills UMC friends for your prayers, my students, I appreciate your trust.

Thank you to the faculty and staff at the U of M for your support and guidance, I have learned so much from all of you: Kristina, Lynn, Richard, Jennifer, Mike, Liz, Fong, J.B., and many others I may be forgetting.

Most of all, thank you Jason for your patience, being at my side, holding my hand, and not letting me quit, you are my bestest bestie. I am very much looking forward to the journey ahead of us.

Lastly, thank you, God, for seeing me through this experience. May all the difficult lessons of my past be transformed into something truly beautiful.

Table of Contents

Chapter 1: Introduction *1*

Chapter 2: Definition of Terms and Methodology *4*

Chapter 3: Learning Lessons in Adversity *18*

Chapter 4: ACE and How We Understand Brain Development *37*

Chapter 5: Acting Out *53*

Chapter 6: Assessment of Executive Function *80*

Chapter 7: Living Dual Lives *99*

Chapter 8: Resilience: Protective Factors *137*

Chapter 9: Behavior Intervention *152*

Chapter 10: Conclusion *187*

Final Reflections *191*

References *193*

Chapter 1: Introduction

Why do some children thrive while other children struggle? Is there a correlation with the amount of trauma and adversity a child is exposed to in their formative years?

More than two-thirds of student referrals, suspensions, and detentions are accumulated by a small number of students, especially in urban schools (Greene, 2008). If these same students are continually disciplined for behavior infractions, then clearly the current disciplinary approach is not working. Something must change.

This qualitative autoethnography explores how and why youth succeed and struggle, through the lens of my own successes and struggles. In the following chapters, I narrate and analyze the chapters of my own life as a "bad kid" in pursuit of what might work for students like me. This study functions as a means of advancing trauma-informed education through critical anecdotes, an important effort for grounding the field in real cases and avoiding theoretical vacuums. Autoethnography as an analytical tool places value on the self-reflexive nature of how my personal understanding and experiences with trauma and teaching survival-based children impacts my understanding of my students. I will supplement this qualitative approach with complementary survey data, ACE scores, and resilience scores. These more quantitative records complement the qualitative focus of this study, while also demonstrating the results of an executive function intervention that I conducted with elementary students.

This book is a serious attempt to discover directions for success with trauma and behavior issues in schools. The data and analysis create a portrait of how the experiences of childhood transition into the outcomes of adulthood. Most importantly, by shedding light on the intervention process, we can increase the odds for today's struggling young people.

This study offers a deeper understanding of trauma and resilience to educators, therapists, and caregivers, based on my personal experiences and professional analysis and application. These readers can implement insights from this study to guide young people towards an individual reflection of their experiences. I also hope to inspire other people to engage in their own autoethnography analysis. There is a healing which occurs when we are brave enough to closely examine our past in search for meaning.

In chapter two I lay out the groundwork for looking at trauma, indicative behavior, skill development, and increased resilience through reviewing important terms and concepts from research and theory on resilience, executive function and behavior interventions. The rest of the book alternates between memoir and analysis chapters. In chapter three, I use memoir narrative to expose my earliest memories of the traumas and adverse experiences that I encountered as a young child. In chapter four, I analyze the previous chapter's experiences through focusing explicitly on adverse experiences and development. In the chapter five I revisit the adolescent years of my life, and then in chapter six I examine those behaviors through the lens of executive function. In chapter seven, I narrate my later teenage years while chapter eight features analysis of those experiences from a perspective of resilience. Finally, in chapter nine I offer brief vignettes of my experience as an educator working with struggling students, revealing how my adverse childhood experiences, executive function, and resilience have impacted my teaching. Through details of the intervention that I developed and implemented, I highlight the importance of designing individual interventions that encompass experiential personal reflection and skill development in an effort to increase long-term resilience.

Chapter 2: Definition of Terms and Methodology

This chapter introduces and defines the various terms and basic behavioral intervention methods used to reach K-12 students who suffer from the effects of Adverse Childhood Experiences (ACEs), and then describes my methodology for this book. In this first section, I cover how trauma affects students in traditional education programs, and then explore definitions of resilience, executive function and behavior interventions.

In this book, I refer to research across various fields of science from brain development to trauma experts. Each source was chosen based on how it resonates with my memoir. Simply put, this science feels right to me and my experiences, though I cannot guarantee that the generalizations will transfer to others. As an authoethnographer, my goal is a deeper understanding of my own case rather than a transferable diagnosis. I want to help teachers understand how trauma affects brain development, alters executive function, and how we can design classroom intervention that promotes long-term resilience in learning.

There is a growing understanding of the relationships between toxic stress, brain development, health, learning, and behavior in the early years (Masten A. S., 2012). Trauma and adverse childhood experiences (ACEs) are correlated with a lack of brain development, as shown by researchers like Masten (2012) and Shonkoff (2012). Specifically, these studies point to an effect on the prefrontal cortex, or the area of the brain that directs executive functions and self-regulation. When a student who has been exposed to high levels of trauma is expected to perform normally, they are less able to do so because their brain has developed differently due to these early experiences. This results in extreme classroom behaviors such as withdrawal and defiance (Massachusetts Advocates for Children, 2005). Students who have undergone these experiences and suffered this level of toxic stress are in what Shonkoff calls "survival mode" (2012).

Due to the connection between toxic stress, brain development, health, learning, and behavior, the sorts of interventions that reduce adversity can also strengthen physical and mental health (Greenberg, 2006). Attempting to improve one area in isolation may not work. Classroom teachers, then, should design behavior interventions which take all factors into account when attempting to increase the resilience of a student in survival mode and reduce the explosive behaviors the student exhibits in the classroom. Teachers and intervention designers must first develop an understanding of trauma, resilience, and executive function, all defined below.

Trauma

Trauma is not the event itself, but rather the response to a stressful experience, causing a person's ability to cope to be dramatically undermined. Lenore Terr defines childhood trauma as the impact of external forces that "render the young person temporarily helpless and break past ordinary coping and defensive operation. This includes not only those conditions marked by intense surprise but also those marked by prolonged and sickening anticipation (1991, p. 11). Herman concurs by stating traumatic events "overwhelm the ordinary human adaptations to life…They confront human beings with the extremities of helplessness and terror (1997, p. 33). Every traumatic experience is different, and the range is broad, including, neglect, abuse, abandonment, and devastating loss. Each child's experience is unique depending on their individual coping skills, resources and the context in which the stress occurs.

Resilience

Resilience refers to the capability of students to do well despite a high level of adverse childhood experiences (ACEs). Resilience is often linked to discussions on change, transition, disaster and adversity. Resilience is how we view the human organism's ability to adapt. This stress-resistant personal quality permits one to thrive despite adversity (Ahern, Ark, & Byers, 2008). Although there is controversy among scholars as to whether resilience is a characteristic, a process, or an outcome, the construct has been characterized by many researchers as a dynamic process among factors that may mediate between an individual, his or her environment, and an outcome (Ahern, Ark, & Byers, 2008).

Developmental resilience studies provide a valuable perspective on the growth-enhancing impact of protective factors and the strengths-based variables that might work against risk (Malekoff, 2004). Bandura's (1994) work stresses that cooperative learning strategies have the dual outcome of improving both self-efficacy and academic achievement. Encouraging students to be diligent in forethought develops their self-regulation and self-reflectiveness about their capabilities, quality of functioning, and the meaning and purpose of their life pursuits. Therefore, while resilience may not be a teachable skill, other related skills such as metacognition, self-regulation, self-efficacy, and self-reflectiveness can be improved and therefore contribute to a higher level of resilience in an individual. These are all executive function skills.

Executive Function

Executive function, the part of the brain damaged by trauma, has several components. Self-reflectiveness, a key component of resilience, is closely related to metacognition, which falls under the bracket of executive function. The term metacognition was introduced by Flavell (1976) to refer to 'the individual's own awareness and consideration of his or her cognitive processes and strategies'. It refers to that uniquely human capacity of people to be self-reflexive, to think about their own thinking and knowing. Metacognition is crucial to helping children understand on a conscious level, and gain mastery and control over their learning. This learning hinges on negotiations of meaning with others through dialogue and conversations. While these conversations can exist internally, they are much more effective in pairs or small groups where multiple perspectives and interpretations can be explored (Fisher, 1998). This reflective process is lacking in students who exhibit severe behavior problems in school.

In addition to self-reflection, children need the ability to process boundaries among community systems in each individual child's life. Students who are lacking metacognitive skills also struggle to negotiate the grey areas within boundaries. Bronfenbrenner identified levels of systems in community in his ecology of human development, a "nested arrangement of concentric structures, each contained within the next" (1979). The model displays the level of interactions between the following systems: individual, family, school, peer, church, neighborhood (mesosystem), then even further outward into the (exosystem) government, media, industry, etc. (see figure 2.1). Strengthening metacognitive skills promotes a student's ability to reflect on appropriateness of interactions across boundary systems.

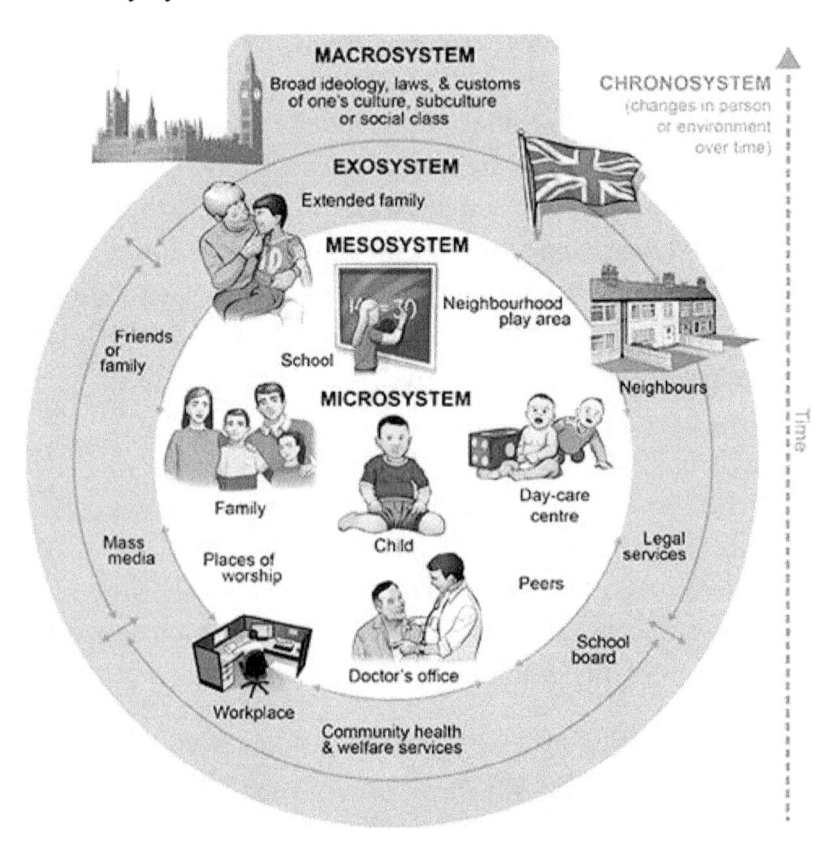

MACROSYSTEM
Broad ideology, laws, & customs of one's culture, subculture or social class

CHRONOSYSTEM
(changes in person or environment over time)

EXOSYSTEM
Extended family

MESOSYSTEM
Neighbourhood play area
School
Friends or family
Neighbours

MICROSYSTEM
Family
Child
Day-care centre
Mass media
Places of worship
Peers
Legal services
Doctor's office
School board
Workplace
Community health & welfare services

Time

Figure 2.1. Bronfrenbrenner's Ecology of Human Development Model, *Fostering Adoption Research in Practice,* Retrieved April 26, 2016, from http://fosteringandadoption.rip.org.uk/topics/child-development/

Behavioral Interventions

Survival-based students are likely to exhibit explosive behaviors in the classroom and require specific behavior interventions in attempt to correct the behavior. In his model for collaborative problem solving, Greene (2008) declared, "Kids do well, if they can" (p. 162). His article claims that behavior challenges result in students who lack the skills to act appropriately and achieve in school. Greene described his philosophy that students who act out require caring adults who will help them determine the lagging skills they must develop to become strong achievers, rather than traditional discipline. This is crucial to urban education where referral rates are much higher than in suburban or rural areas and traditional discipline plans are failing. If the current form of school discipline was working, students in survival mode wouldn't be losing valuable learning opportunities while receiving punishments. Therefore, the first step to re-establishing urban education is to seek alternatives to school discipline and the usual classroom management.

In addition, the discipline problems so common among urban children are directly correlated to the generational oppression in minority families being exposed to higher levels of trauma, stress, and abuse. Children have an increased likelihood of acting out in explosive ways in school when escalated by the power struggles inherent to traditional discipline approaches, such as authoritarian practices, in which the authority is always correct and there is little room for discussion and reflection surrounding the unwanted behavior. Student behaviors are explosive because students often feel powerless and subordinate to the teachers and the traditional classroom management approach is that students must be controlled and forced to learn.

However, these students are acting out because certain basic needs are not being met. In *The Classroom of Choice,* Erwin writes that Glasser's Lead Management Theory moves away from the notion that students must be manipulated, controlled, and forced to learn. Instead, he draws on Maslow's Hierarchy, examination of basic needs, persuasion and problem solving as the central components of this theory (Erwin, 2004). Both Glasser and Greene agree students are competent young people who are responsible for their own education, and the teacher should really be a facilitator who shares the power with the students by including them in decisions as to how the structure of their learning environment should be set up, with the teacher inviting student input on every facet of the course.

Research Goals and Questions

Students who have experienced high level of ACEs demonstrate a deficit in executive function and self-regulation. Therefore, when asked to do classroom activities which require these skills, they simply cannot, because their brains are not wired to do so. As teachers it is nearly impossible for us to reduce the level of toxic stress that students face at home. However, we can promote executive function and self-regulation in the classroom through interventions that focus on addressing student needs through not continuing a cycle of trauma but rather giving metacognitive support and power to students. The rest of this book will delve into the methods and theories of executive function and self-regulation in action, and how I and my students have mastered them and taken control of our futures. I will seek to answer the following research questions:

How can I, as a teacher and as a student who has experienced adverse traumatic experiences, understand and improve student behavior, executive function, and resilience?

How do my experiences as teacher and student impact my understanding of students with behavior problems?

How did I become a resilient learner and how does that affect how I interact with students as a teacher?

Can negative classroom behaviors be decreased through an intervention intended to improve the executive function in students?

How do interventions influence student learning in a classroom setting?

How did the impact of the adverse experiences I encountered relate to the explosive behaviors I exhibited?

Methodology

I choose to answer these questions through autoethnography. Autoethnography is the study of one's own culture and oneself as a part of that culture in many variations (Patton, 2002). This study in particular addresses elementary classroom culture and the childhood trauma that influences it. As an autoethnographic researcher I will be studying myself and my understanding of students—specifically those who have high adverse experiences and find learning difficult and act out in the classroom. Their culture is my own, as I too experienced high levels of trauma and acted out in school. I am examining the student culture of trauma and adverse experiences through my identities as a researcher, as teacher of these students, and as a previous student with my own memories of childhood trauma and classroom behavior problems. Ultimately, I am an educator in search of solutions in my classroom environment. Therefore, at this level of exploratory research it is beneficial to examine my own experiences alongside my role working with students who have experienced trauma. I share those experiences so as to give critical insight to other classroom teachers who may not share that background.

Within educational research, there is a growing trend and appreciation for studies that encompass the researcher's voice throughout the process. These narratives are becoming prominent evaluative material. Autoethnography unites these trends in which the author and the subject are interchangeable; the result is an imaginative and insightful published work (Muncey, 2010, pp. xii-xiii). Autoethnographic narratives take the form of both telling and showing. Telling analytically explores issues which underpin the approach; showing uses examples from the narrative to evoke the reader to engage in their own imaginative relationship with the text (Muncey, 2010, p. xiii).

Autoethnography is "an autobiographical genre of writing research that displays multiple layers of consciousness, connecting the personal to the cultural" (Ellis & Bochner, 2000, p. 739). To delve deeper into the idea of multiple layers, Reed-Danahay suggest another definition: "an ethnography includes the researcher's vulnerable self, emotions, body and spirit and produces evocative stories that create the effect of reality and seeks fusion between social science and literature" (Reed-Danahay, 1997). Muncey stresses the importance of considering the kind of filter that the researcher will utilize to separate personal experience from the subject of study. It is impossible to separate the impact of personal experience, and therefore is essential to accept oneself as the focus of the study. Autoethnography is a research that privileges the individual by "attempting to portray an individual experience in a way that evokes the imagination of the reader" (Muncey, 2010, p. 2).

According to Wolcott, Ethnography is a branch of qualitative research which relies on "Participant Observation Strategies" (Wolcott, 2001, p. 90). The autoethnographer rests on this branch as not only are they a participant in the social context of their experience, but they are also an observer of their own story and its social location (Muncey, 2010, p. 2). Most autoethnographers at first do not intend to use autoethnography as a method, but later resort to it as a way of communicating complex feelings and experiences which cannot simply be shared in conventional ways. Phenomenology closely resonates as it carries a similar purpose of portraying a "lived experience."
Phenomenologists infer that life is separated by everyday life and provinces of meaning, where we reflect on everyday life.

In other words, the difference between the meaning of life, and finding meaning in life. Autoethnography goes deeper as the researcher must recognize there is no distinction between conducting research and living life when the autoethnographer is both the researcher and the researched (Muncey, 2010).

In order to be understood as an individual it is important to consider self-reflexivity. This sense of self is comprised of biology, social context, and consciousness. An important part of self-contained in the private thoughts, feelings, and perceptions that are communicated only when chosen. Reflexive self-awareness is integral to being human. Concerns about self-reflexive research most often regard the blurred relationships between the researchers and researched, which could pose an issue in terms of reliability and validity (Borbasi, 1994). However, this capacity of self-reflexiveness awards the opportunity to see the self in our experiences, and the self as others view us. Different perspectives emerge as we consider our personal world as if it were someone else's, and someone else's personal world as our own. This provides the capacity for empathy and openness (Muncey, 2010). To really understand oneself, we must consider how others view us. According to Mead, the sense of self transforms our relation to the world and awards us unique character. In viewing our self as an object, we can perceive others and interact with ourselves, which yield influence on the world (Mead, 1934). This promotes the self to become a reflexive process. Romanyshyn (1982) extends this idea that consciousness in not experienced in our heads, rather is constructed by reflections of thoughts, feelings through the people and things who make up our world.

Muncey points out the need to consider the subjective awareness which provides a framework for viewing the characteristics of the personal world constructed by the researcher. When personal world is combined with bodily experiences, it makes our experiences seem vulnerable and transparent. This explains why individuals prefer to internalize rather than outwardly communicate perceptions. This sheds light on the suppression of traumatic memories. While writing this early chapter, I fully anticipate reliving my own trauma as I portray the story in authentic detail. However, I seek the value in searching for meaning and coherence in my life in order to offer direction for others. My readers can begin to understand when they can imagine themselves in my world.

I believe that using an autoethnographic lens will help to broaden and deepen ongoing conversations pertaining to educating students who have faced trauma because I provide both sides: my role as a student, and then as a teacher. Tami Spry (2001) suggests that human experience is messy and chaotic and what divides autoethnography from typical autobiographies is the researcher's intent to subvert a dominant discourse. It therefore becomes "a self-narrative that critiques the situations of self with others in social contexts" (Spry, p. 710).

However, I recognize the limitations of this very personal and qualitative method. Therefore, I triangulate these personal reflections with document analysis, ACE and resilience scores, and survey data collected during and after an intervention with 20 students selected from the fourth and fifth grades at an urban elementary school in Minnesota. I will examine data from a 25-week behavior intervention for these students, intended to target the deficit in executive function, problem solving skills, and self-regulation. I anticipate that this combination of autoethnography and document/survey analysis will allow me to reflect on which elements used in this behavior intervention were the most effective, while incorporating a constant self-reflexive conversation of my own experiences working with the students as their teacher and living with my experiences as a survival-based student.

Data Collection and Analysis

Due to the autoethnographic approach, my primary source of data is my own childhood. Data collection will take the form of recollection through memoir. As a former kid in the juvenile system, I overcame a difficult childhood, encountering many adverse experiences. In this study I will reflect on my experiences, both as a survival-based youth who was able to overcome adversity, and, as professional educating students who are facing similar difficulties. As an educator in both formal and non-formal settings over the past fifteen years, I have much professional experience to draw upon. I will then analyze this data through a self-reflexive lens, using codes from existing research to organize and interpret my memoir chapters.

In the final chapter, I will also examine vignettes from my teaching career and preexisting data from the twenty-five-week behavior intervention program. Through combining my childhood and professional experience with the literature and my doctorate coursework, I developed this behavior intervention to administer to my students. As a more formal data collection method, this intervention requires more description.

In Chapter 9, I refer to the results of this intervention. I use observation notes and my personal reflections recorded in the process of choosing intervention strategies based on research readings, experience working with the students on a daily basis, and my past experiences as a student. Drawing from these notes, I assemble vignettes in effort to share these stories. All of this data will, for the purpose of this study, be used from the perspective of my experience as a teacher and individual and how I perceived it working for my students. Analysis will involve identifying common themes between my own life experiences and my impression of the intervention's effectiveness with my students.

This book adds to the body of research on trauma informed education and will provide a greater understanding the relationship between resilience and executive function. Researchers like Masten (2012) point out the need for further investigation in this area to address the needs of improving student learning and resilience in the classroom. Using autoethnography to examine this culture provides an in-depth reflection of a classroom teacher's account of an applied behavior intervention which can be reflected on by other teachers, among other applications.

Chapter 3: Learning Lessons in Adversity

From my earliest memories, I can remember my parents had huge arguments. I learned what it meant to walk on eggshells pretty much the day after I learned how to walk. Even as a little girl, I could feel tension between my parents. Things would be calm and then they would erupt into a blowout. Their voices would rise, bad words would fly, and I learned that was my cue to run and hide. I slipped under the nearest bed or hid deep in a closet while my parents fought violently inside our trailer house. Were they mad at me? Was I in trouble? I never really knew, but I didn't emerge until I no longer heard them arguing.

I remember one time when our house literally looked like a tornado had gone through. Broken pieces and debris cluttered the floor, shredded pictures lined the trash can, and the cupboard had a hole the size of a fist. It was hard to know what was happening, but I remember the sick feeling in my stomach, the fear that somehow this mess was my fault. As far back as I can remember there were events in life that scared me.

My dad was a farmer, so he had a flexible, yet busy, work schedule. From the moment I was potty trained, I had daddy daycare while Mom went to work as a seamstress at a garment factory. My parents established our home on my grandparents' farm. Between Dad, Grandma, and Grandpa there was always someone to look after me. Unless, of course, they each assumed someone else was keeping an eye on me. In that case, I spent many days wandering around the farm playing with the animals and questioning the sheer miracle of nature as I watched the crops grow taller than me, witnessed the animals giving birth, and snatched the delicious vegetables growing in Grandma's extravagant garden.

"Bon, let's go to town!" I heard Dad yelling for me, his strong voice carrying over the farm. I went running, knowing we were leaving for another adventure. I never knew where we were headed, but my dad took me just about everywhere he went. When I reached his old Chevy truck, Dad would reach down, scoop me up, and toss me in the driver's side. I crawled over to the other side. Some days we went to the John Deere store to get parts for the tractor. Some days it was to the welding store, farm supply store, feed store, or an auction. It didn't matter. I loved hanging out with my dad. I knew every trip to town meant running errands and the usual stop at Dairy Queen before heading back to the farm so Dad could get back to his field work.

I helped in the field, too. On each tractor, I had my designated spot. On some tractors, I had a little seat next to Dad. On the older tractors without a cab, Dad poked my little legs under the armrest so that I sat backward in the seat while he sat forward. For hours I rode with Dad on the tractor watching my little feet dangling, feeling the wind blow through my sun-bleached blonde hair, and counting the rows behind us. In the afternoon, Dad took his coat and placed it on the tractor floor. I lay down for my nap right there under Dad's feet. It was amazing fun for a little girl nearly three years old. I always had a dark farmer's tan on my arms from being out in the hot sun all summer. I was a farm girl. Life to me was pleasant and peaceful for the most part, with the exception of my parents' frequent violent outrages.

When my dad wasn't busy with farm chores, he and my uncle worked on my dad's race car. Saturday nights were race nights for my family. Dad loaded up the car, Grandma popped popcorn for us to sneak in, and we headed across the road to the local racetrack. It was super loud and the wind blew the dirt from the track in my face, but I loved watching my dad race. My dad could have been famous for as much of a hero he was to me.

Once in a while, my "friends" came over to play during the day. For hours when my dad was gone out in the field, the three girls and I let our imaginations run wild, dreaming up a whole new world. Then one day the games started to change. We started playing games like house and doctor—games that made me feel really silly and weird inside. When we played house, each family member took turns humping each other. If you didn't know how, you could practice on a pillow or blanket.

In order to see the doctor, you had to take your pants off. The doctor would come in and "clean" your private parts. The doctor used parts cleaner: a gasoline and mineral spirits solution mechanics use to clean car parts. It burned a little when the doctor splashed it on and rubbed it inside me. It burned between my legs. Then the doctor would wipe it around with the dirty rag. Finally, the doctor would start to lick the cleaned area.

"Do you want to be a doctor when you grow up, Bonnie?"

"They make a lot of money!"

"Here! You try. Let's see if you will make a good doctor!"

Each of us took turns being the doctor or the patient. It seemed really scary to me, but I was only five years old and my friends several years older. I remember feeling icky, really icky. Somehow this felt very wrong, but as a little girl I wasn't quite sure. This went on for an entire summer. Most days it was just one "friend" that wanted to play these silly games, several days all three of us played. I never told anyone.

My little brother was born in July. I started kindergarten that fall, and a month later my mom told me we were moving to town. She gave me a big box and told me to pack all my toys. I knew I would miss the farm, but I was really excited to have a new house. It wasn't until I unpacked my toys in my new room that I realized Dad wasn't moving with us.

Mom and Dad got divorced just after I started kindergarten. After spending almost every day with my dad for nearly five years, it was really hard for me not seeing him. My dad and I were buddies, and I was afraid I had done something wrong so I couldn't see him anymore.

I only saw my dad on weekends, and those weekends were scarce. When I did see him, he usually picked up my brother and me on Friday night and dropped me off at the church on Sunday morning for Sunday school. Mom picked me up after. I had been attending Sunday school every

Sunday since my mom enrolled me after I was potty trained. After the divorce, she still insisted I go. My dad dropped me off at the church so I could attend. Sunday school was okay, so I didn't mind. But not being able to spend Sunday with my dad made the weekend visits incredibly short.

While searching for a boyfriend, my mom went out on many dates, leaving my brother and me home with babysitters. There was one babysitter whom I never really liked much. Mostly because she taught me to play games that made me feel the same silliness that I had felt just two years earlier. In these games, she would put things inside of me. I told my mom about it this time, because I felt so icky. I was really scared to tell my mom because I thought I would get in trouble. I had never told her about any of the other times that I had played games that made me feel silly.

I don't remember my mom really saying much about it, but she asked me lots of questions. Later that night I heard her talking to the babysitter's mom about what I said. That girl never came to baby-sit me and my brother again.

Within two years, my mom had a serious boyfriend who moved in with us. I never really liked him much. He wasn't my dad, and I missed my dad a lot. Mom's boyfriend was usually crabby, and I always felt scared around him. Whenever he got angry, he would spank me a lot—harder and longer than my dad had ever spanked me. The worst of all, he drank a lot. There was rarely a time when we didn't have a bottle of Bacardi or case of Diet Coke in our house. I can vividly remember the fridge being near empty with the exception of the case of Diet Coke.

"We are on a tight budget," mom would tell us.

"How tight is a budget that affords Diet Coke over food?" I would angrily mutter under my breath.

One of the best gifts my dad ever gave me for Christmas was a bike. But it wasn't just any bike. It was a mountain bike. This was long ago, when I was in second grade, when mountain bikes were first introduced. None of my friends had ever seen a bike like this, with wide tires and straight handlebars. Until the new mountain style, ten-speeds were somewhat dainty with thin tires and curvy handle bars. With the newest bike in town, I was sure to be the coolest kid in school! The shiny new bike was my Christmas gift from my dad. I could hardly wait to ride it. I would come home from school and ride it around in the garage. I was waiting for the day the Minnesota winter would give way, the snow would melt, and I could head out on my new bike. Every time I saw my dad he would ask,

"Have you been riding your new bike?"

Sadly, I would answer, "No, Mom said I can't ride it in the snow."

"Well, I got the kind with the wide tires so you can ride it anytime, Bon," Dad explained.

I was never sure which parent I was supposed to listen to, Dad or Mom. Dad seemed disappointed I wasn't enjoying my new bike, but I lived with Mom. After all, my mom had told me I couldn't ride my bike on the streets when the roads were icy. So, I waited.

Finally, a nice day came! As I was getting ready for school, brushing my hair, putting on my clothes, I looked outside and saw the neighbor riding his bike to school.

"The roads must be okay to ride bikes, not too icy," I thought to myself. "Today is the day!"

I finished getting ready, grabbed my backpack, hopped on my bike, and headed off to school. All of my classmates thought my new bike was the coolest. I was so proud. I rode it home after school and put it back in its spot in the garage.

When Mom got home from work, one of the first things she asked me was, "Your bike is wet. Why did you ride your bike in the snow?"

"Dad told me I could ride it, and I saw the neighbor ride his, so I thought it was okay," I responded. Mom didn't really say much else about it.

Later that night, when the boyfriend got home, I got the usual spankings. He always worked late, so he got home about 2:00 or 3:00 a.m. He always smelled bad, like old booze, and dirt, and looked greasy. My bedroom door flew open, the light snapped on, and his loud, quick footsteps approached my bed. He reached down, ripped the covers off me with so much force that my blankets landed on the floor across the room. He grabbed me, threw me on my stomach, and started spanking me.

He kept spanking me over and over again, sometimes missing, hitting my back, other times slapping my legs. It hurt so badly. I screamed and cried, waking my little brother who shared the bedroom with me. He started crying. The boyfriend just kept spanking me, so hard and for what felt like forever. I knew he was done when his loud, quick footsteps returned to the door and he snapped off the light and slammed the door. I lay in my bed, shaking and sore, sometimes nearly breathless. I got up and tip-toed over to my little brother.

"Shh! Shh! It's okay. Stop crying before we get in trouble! Shh! Shh!" I hugged him, praying that he stopped crying so the boyfriend didn't come back. Then I found my blankets on the floor where they had landed, went back to bed, and quietly cried myself to sleep.

Mostly I was never quite sure why I was getting the spankings, because the boyfriend rarely ever said anything. He came in, spanked me, and left. Where was my mom? Sleeping? Why wasn't she spanking me? This time I was able to figure out that I was in trouble for riding my bike to school in the snow, because the next day my bike wasn't in the garage. It had been carried down to the basement of our house. I knew I wouldn't be riding it for a long time. I told my dad how I had gotten in trouble for riding my bike and he was really mad, but somehow it seemed that there was never anything my dad could do. Didn't he realize how bad things were at Mom's house?

I always wondered why my mom rarely punished me. It was always the boyfriend. If my mom got mad at me, she grabbed my arm and pinched it, slapped me, or pulled my hair. One time, when I stole a little toy car from one of my classmates, his mom called our house. I lied because I was so scared of getting the spankings. I tried to run in the other room, but my mom chased after me, knocked me down, sat on top of me, and started hitting me, whipping me back and forth until my shirt ripped.

"You're a terrible, rotten, bad kid," she yelled. Late that night, I got more spankings from the boyfriend.

I grew to really resent him. Why did this guy who wasn't my dad keep spanking me? On the top of our entertainment center where nearly two dozen trophies that the boyfriend had earned from wrestling in High school. When my mom made me help clean the house, I had to dust each of his dumb trophies. I wanted to throw them out the window. Each trophy reminded me of his strength and how much it hurt to get the spankings.

My brother, Bruce, was a little more than five years younger than me. For whatever reason, it took him forever to be potty trained. One night when he was four years old, he got the spankings. It started at bedtime. I was trying to help the little guy get on his pajamas and nighttime diaper. He had outgrown his pajamas and they were a little tight, so we were having trouble getting them on. He was tired, fussy, and whiny. I tried to keep him quiet so we didn't get in trouble, but it didn't work.

Soon the boyfriend stumbled down the hallway and came in our room. He reeked of stale booze and cigarettes. He grabbed my brother, just a little guy by his arm, and started spanking him. Bruce was screaming and squirming. The boyfriend bounced him back and forth from his bed to mine. I thought his little arm was going to come out of the socket. I wanted to stop it, but I was too scared of getting hit myself, so I stayed still on my side of the room. My brother endured spanking after spanking.

Finally, for the first time ever, my mom came in our room during the spankings.

She yelled at her boyfriend, telling him, "That's enough. You're going to hurt him! Stop! That's enough!"

Her boyfriend didn't stop. The diaper I had just put on my little brother was falling to shreds from all the hard spankings. Finally, it was over. My mom stayed and tried to quiet down Bruce. *Why didn't she ever tell her boyfriend to stop when he was spanking me?* That was the question on my mind as I went to bed that night.

I always felt so scared. Scared of getting in trouble. Scared of being hit. Eventually the spankings tapered off, but there were still the unpredictable times I got a slap or thunk on the head, or the most dreaded hair yank. My Sunday school teacher had told me to pray when I was scared. At night I said my prayers before bed. I asked God to take the boyfriend away from us:

"Please, God, let him die in a car accident on the way home tonight so he can't hurt us anymore."

Every week in Sunday school, I learned more about God. I was so curious about God. He sounded so amazing, but I wondered why he allowed such bad things to happen. I learned that God answered prayers, but I wondered why he didn't answer mine. I believed God could make me strong and courageous, so why did I feel so scared?

Sometimes I went to school with bruises. When the teacher asked about them, I lied, saying I fell. One day in third grade I was called into the principal's office, where a lady and a man were waiting for me with a camera. They told me they were from social services and they heard about some bruises on my arms. They came to take pictures and ask me some questions. I was so scared of getting in trouble if I told them the truth.

"It's okay, Bonnie. You can tell us, and we are going to make sure you are safe," they kept reassuring me. I told them about a few things going on at home, about the spankings, and how I felt scared a lot. It was about that time that I started to see a counselor and the spankings seemed to stop for a while.

I hated going to see the counselor. He asked me the same questions over and over again, "How does that make you feel? How do you feel about that?" I was crying! Couldn't he tell I was sad? My mom always complained about taking off of work to bring me to see him. The only thing I liked about going there was the cool toys they had in the waiting room that my brother and I played with while my mom took her turn talking with the counselor.

I remember seeing several different counselors when I was growing up. There were the ones Mom took me to see and counselors who came to the house. I also had a big sister for Big Brothers/Big Sisters and a school social worker. The big sister and the school social workers were my favorites. I liked talking to them and got excited for my appointments, but the counselors were all just as boring. Of all that counseling, I'm not sure any even helped. I don't remember feeling any better. What a waste of good playtime.

The spankings weren't the only thing I dreaded. On occasion my mom and her boyfriend got into huge fights. It reminded me of the fights Mom and Dad had, when I got scared and ran to hide. I thought the tornados would be gone after my parents divorced because my mom promised me no more fighting. The tornados still happened. I remember coming out of my room to see things scattered everywhere. In my mom's room, the dresser was lying on its side and the legs were broke off. There was a big hole that had been punched into the wall. If I looked closely, I could find streaks of dried blood.

"Are you okay?" I asked my mom.

"Yes, but he left," she cried quietly.

"Good!" I thought. *"God was protecting us!"*

About a week later, the boyfriend and his garbage bags full of clothes came back. The hole in the wall stayed there for a while. Soon there was another hole to match.

One particular morning, my mom had already left for work and took my brother to daycare. The house was empty except for me and the boyfriend, who was still asleep. As I was getting ready for school, brushing my hair and getting dressed, I remembered that Mom had told me to call my dad before school. Sometimes my dad was hard to reach and I had been leaving him several messages, so Mom had told me to try again that morning.

After I made the call, I went back to my room and finished getting ready. The boyfriend appeared in my doorway. My stomach turned hard as he started yelling at me and I remembered thinking, *"Please not the spankings!"* He just stood there and yelled, saying bad words. As his temper flared, he hit my bedroom door twice, leaving two large hand-size holes. My mom put a poster on the door to cover the holes. Ironically, the picture on the poster was an oversized heart that hid the violent memory behind. Twelve years passed before that door got replaced.

Other than the fighting, the big thing that bothered me was when Mom and the boyfriend had loud sexual encounters and forgot to shut the door. It was difficult for me to have to hear that. It reminded me of the silly games I had been forced to play. Sometimes my brother woke and I tried to keep him quiet. He was an inquisitive toddler at four years of age. I feared if he bothered them, we would both get the spankings.

Two of my favorite activities when I was young were 4-H and Adventure Club. Adventure Club was a Wednesday night church program at the Baptist church in our town. Nearly two-thirds of the elementary school children in our small town attended every week. I had always gone to the Lutheran church for Sunday school, but this was always the best part of my life. In Sunday school, we talked a lot about different Bible stories and prayer and God. At Adventure Club, I started to learn about Jesus. We always sang fun songs and the adults had a ton of energy to play with us and put on cheeky skits. It made me so excited to learn about faith. One night when we were singing a song about being a

Christian, the song leader stopped the song and explained to us what it meant to be a Christian. She told us that all you had to do was ask Jesus into your heart. I decided that I wanted to do that, so I prayed quietly, "Jesus, please come into my heart."

4-H was a ten-year journey. I joined 4-H when I was in third grade. The meetings were slightly boring, but I loved taking projects to the county fair. Sewing was my best project, although it caused many outrageous arguments between my mom and me. Mom was an extreme perfectionist when it came to sewing, and she made me rip my seams out when they were only slightly crooked. I hated picking out the seams. Even a few stitches off and I had to rip them out. However, I learned to be very good at sewing.

Unfortunately, my sexuality was exposed prematurely. It was a combination of the silly games and hearing Mom and the boyfriend when they had sex. Another time I found the boyfriend's box of magazines, all of them showing naked women. I thought that must be what boys like to see. Always hoping to fit in at school, I snuck some of the magazines into my backpack and passed them out to a few of my third-grade classmates. I fit in, that's for sure—until the principal found out. That night I suffered the worst level of spankings ever.

I'll never forget the day I learned what suicide was. I was only in third grade. Taking a shortcut to school one morning, I rounded the corner of my neighbors' house, reaching the point in the alley where I could see the backside of their house. It was then I saw the body. The neighbor boy was in his early twenties, I was told. I knew him only from the car he drove, the one he parked out front of his home, signifying his presence. Nearly every morning I had walked past his car on the way to school.

At first, I wasn't quite sure what I was seeing. I stood there peering across the open yard, trying to decode what I was looking at. There he was, hanging from the deck with what looked like a belt tied around his neck. I looked up and down several times noticing his feet as they dangled. Below him was a small patio table toppled over on its side. *Why was he hanging there? Was he dead? What should I do? Do I call 9-1-1? Was this an emergency? I will keep walking to school and tell a teacher.*

I took a few more steps down the alley. I heard a car pull up in the front of the house and heard two doors close. Two policemen walked around the side of the house. I walked a little further, hoping they wouldn't see me. I continued to watch from a distance as they talked to each other. I couldn't make out what they were saying. Soon they laid out a big black bag. They worked together as they lowered the body to the ground. I didn't stay to see the rest. I knew I needed to get to school.

A few hours after class started our teacher talked to us about the death in our small community. I was curious about suicide, which was the word the teacher used to describe the death. My mind raced with questions. *Did it hurt to die like that? Why did he do that? Was he sad? How could anyone be so sad that they would want to die? Will I ever be that sad?*

My third-grade teacher was the worst teacher in all my years of school. Somewhere between me bringing the magazines to school and asking lots of questions about the suicide, she seemed very irritated with me. Many times, she would be very harsh in the way she talked to me and most often gave me very stern looks. Obviously, she thought I was a bad kid. Perhaps I was the most challenging student she ever had. When the year was over, I was convinced my life could only get better.

Overall, third grade was one of the hardest years for me. I was exposed to so many things at such an early age. To be exposed to porn and suicide brought on huge life lessons that no third grader should ever learn so young. The following summer, my mom's stroke gave our family another challenge. I was forced to grow up fast. I never knew what was coming next, but I began to accept that crazy things happened in my house and that was just the way it was.

When summer came, I got to spend more time on the farm helping my dad. Bruce and I usually spent all weekend with my dad since I didn't go to Sunday school in the summer. One special Saturday was an exception, because my mom and I were going to see a play in town, *The Wizard of Oz*. It was the first play I would see, and I was really excited to go out with my mom. I felt like a big girl. The plan was to help my dad on the farm during the day and in the afternoon, I was to shower and get ready so Mom could pick me up. Bruce would stay with Dad. I helped Dad all day and when it was time.

I said, "I'm going to go shower, Dad, and get ready."

"That's not necessary, Bon. Your mom is not coming," my dad said.

I started to argue with my dad; obviously he didn't understand that we had this plan.

"Your mom is in the hospital. She won't be coming," he sternly repeated and walked away.

WHAT? This can't be right. No way. I ran to the house and called my mom's house. The phone rang and rang, but Mom never picked up. The whole time Bruce had no idea what was going on. I tried to explain to him but he didn't understand.

Two days later, Bruce and I were taken to my aunt and uncle's house. It was then I was told my mom was in the hospital because she had suffered a stroke. I wasn't sure what it meant, but we knew she was going to be there for a while. Bruce and I were shuffled from one family member to the next for the next eight weeks while my mom remained in the hospital.

Eventually, after my mom was released from intensive care, I was taken to visit her. She had been airlifted to a bigger hospital in the Twin Cities area. I think most family members were reluctant to let me see my mom in the hospital, for fear it was too shocking for a young girl. The blood clot was in the right side of my mom's brain, which meant it paralyzed her left side. The doctors said her stroke was triggered from a combination of smoking and being on birth control pills. My mom was gone for almost the entire summer.

When the county fair came, my mom was still in the hospital. I was glad I had already completed most of my 4-H projects for the fair. My aunt took me to the fair and I met with each project judge. One by one, I showed my projects and expressed my excitement for the creations I had made.

That summer my mind had been cluttered with so many thoughts—everything I experienced in the past year, what my dad was doing, when I could see him, and how I wished my mom could be there at the fair with me. Somehow, amazingly, I pushed every fearful feeling deep down into a secret place and allowed my mind to concentrate only on the details of my projects and focus my attention on answering the challenging questions each judge proposed. I actually did surprisingly well at the fair; for the first time I earned a purple ribbon for my sewing.

At the county fair that year I learned far more than the ability to show my projects. It was then that I learned how to wear a mask. While I sat there talking to the judges, everything about me looked good on the outside. I spoke clearly, explained myself well, and smiled as they complimented my perfectly straight sewing. *If they only knew what I had gone through to accomplish such straight sewing.* On the inside I was so damaged. I missed my dad so much. I was unsure when my mom would be coming home. I wore my mask well, hiding every hurt.

When Mom came home, things were twice as bad because now the left side of her body was paralyzed. Mom had to use a cane to walk. Her speech was slow and slurred. She couldn't drive. And still to this day, she cannot use her left hand. Mom had to learn how to do *everything* with one hand, making simple things like tying shoes or cutting steak impossible. There were many things my mom didn't know how to do with one hand. I helped her with things like shaving her underarms, tying her shoes, making her bed, and zipping her coat.

Recovering from a stroke sent my mom into severe depression. Her self-esteem fell to an ultimate low. She took most of her stress out on me as the oldest, especially when I tried to help her take care of herself or with household tasks. She would yell and scream at me.

"You stupid f_ing brat, you can't do anything right." She would hit me with one hand, or pull my hair.

The boyfriend cracked under the new stress. He left, which felt like a blessing, except that as the oldest, I was now responsible for cleaning the house and taking care of my brother. I also had to cook all the meals for the family. Because Mom couldn't drive, I sometimes had to get the groceries at the store in order to cook the meals. I was only ten years old doing all that I could for my mom, my brother, and myself.

If that wasn't enough, these new changes were hard on my mom's self-esteem. She took her frustrations out on me, yelling at me for everything. I can even remember how she said once, "You are a bastard kid and it is your fault that my boyfriend left." I admit I had been glad when he finally left. He was an abusive alcoholic. But in my heart, I knew it was never my fault he left.

Chapter 4: ACE and How We Understand Brain Development

My early memories in the previous chapter reveal how Adverse Childhood Experiences (ACEs) begin, and the quick impact that they have. In this chapter I draw on research on ACEs to analyze those influences, including how childhood adversity and trauma impact the body and physical alter the brain architecture. Finally, I will define and briefly explore executive function as it relates to inhibitions of the prefrontal cortex and apply this literature to the memoir data.

Nearly five years ago, in the midst of reading article after article for my doctorate coursework, I came across what is commonly called the ACE Study: "Relationship of Childhood Abuse and Household Dysfunction to Many of the Leading Causes of Death in Adults" (Felitti, et al., 1998). The ACE Study was conducted through the Kaiser Permanente and Centers for Disease Control and Prevention in the mid-late 1990s. It was a turning point in my education. For once, research was clear and intriguing, directly applied to my life, and made complete sense.

The ACE Study was conducted from 1995-1997 with more than 17,000 participants. The respondents predominantly represented the middle-upper class demographic; 75 percent Caucasian; 75 percent had attended college; the average age was 57 (Tough, 2012). This study is one of the largest investigations to examine the correlation between childhood trauma and adult mental health and well-being. Participants were given complex physical exams, as well as in-depth questioning about their childhood experiences. The results pinpointed ten major risk factors which lead to later physical and mental illness in adult life.

Of the 10 types of childhood trauma measured in the ACE Study, five are personal: physical abuse, verbal abuse, sexual abuse, physical neglect, and emotional neglect. Five are related to other family members: a parent who's an alcoholic, a mother who's a victim of domestic violence, a family member in jail, a family member diagnosed with a mental illness, and the disappearance of a parent through divorce, death or abandonment. Each type of trauma counts as one point. So, a person who's been physically abused, with one alcoholic parent and a mother who was beaten up has an ACE score of three.

There are, of course, many other types of childhood trauma — watching a sibling being abused, losing a caregiver (grandmother, mother, grandfather, etc.), homelessness, surviving and recovering from a severe accident, witnessing a father being abused by a mother, witnessing a grandmother abusing a father, etc. The ACE Study included only those 10 childhood traumas because those were mentioned as most common by a group of about 300 Kaiser members; those traumas were also well studied individually in the research literature. Similarly, the CDC-Kaiser Permanente Adverse Childhood Experiences Study found that survivors of childhood trauma are up to 5,000% more likely to attempt suicide, have eating disorders, or become IV drug users. (Felitti, et al., 1998)

The previous chapter presents scenarios of adverse childhood experiences that match up to the ACE 10 Question Screening Tool (Figure 2.2):

1. Emotional Abuse: "You're a terrible, rotten, bad kid," she yelled.

2. Physical Abuse: If my mom got mad at me, she grabbed my arm pinching it, slapped me, or pulled my hair. One time, when I stole a little toy car from one of my classmates, his mom called our house. I lied because I was so scared of getting the spankings. I tried to run in the other room, but my mom chased after me, knocked me down, sat on top of me, and started hitting me, whipping me back and forth until my shirt ripped.

3. Sexual Abuse: We started playing games like house and doctor -- games that made me feel really silly and weird inside.

4. Emotional Neglect: Somehow it seemed that there was never anything my dad could do. Didn't he realize how bad things were at Mom's house?

5. Physical Neglect: I can vividly remember the fridge being near empty with the exception of the case of Diet Coke.

6. Parents Divorced: Mom and Dad got divorced just after I started kindergarten.

7. Mother Treated Violently: I slipped under the nearest bed or hid deep in a closet while my parents fought violently inside our trailer house.

8. <u>Alcoholic in the Home:</u> Soon the boyfriend stumbled down the hallway and came in our room. He reeked of stale booze and cigarettes.

9. <u>Chronically Depressed Household Member:</u> Recovering from a stroke sent my mom into severe depression. Her self-esteem fell to an ultimate low.

10. <u>Imprisoned Household Member:</u> Does not apply to my life.

      I fall into the majority with exposure to more than one type of trauma. My life example supports these findings, in that family violence occurred in my home, as well as abuse, neglect, and familial alcoholism. Mom's boyfriend clearly had a drinking problem. The domestic violence between the boyfriend and my mom transferred into abuse and neglect as my mom either took it out on me, or suffered from her own mental disparities to avoid being a neglectful parent. Overall, the situation was a domino effect, or perfect storm of trauma in my life.

      Based on the ACE screening tool, I experienced nine of the ten types of childhood trauma for an ACE score of 9. An ACE score of 4 or higher is considered high risk. Additionally, experiencing other types of toxic stress over months or years increases the risk of health consequences. This certainly explains the numerous health issues I now face as an adult. However, I am not as interested in the original purpose of the ACE study, which was exclusively a predictor of health problems in adulthood.

While originally intended to predict factors in adult physical and mental health, the ACE study is now considered a prominent factor in adolescent brain development which ties closely to executive function. In their technical report, Shonkoff et al. (2012) incorporate integrated knowledge from biological and social sciences to present an ecobiodevelopmental (EBD) framework to "better understand the complex relationships among adverse childhood circumstances, toxic stress, brain architecture, and poor physical and mental health well into adulthood" (p. 233). This EBD framework draws on report from the Center on Developing Child at Harvard University encouraging consideration as to "how childhood adversity can lead to lifelong impairments in learning, behavior, and both physical and mental health" (Shonkoff, Garner, & The Committee on Psychosocial Aspects of the Child and Family Health, p. 233).

Scientists in fields such as neuroendocrinology, stress physiology, and epigenetics are closely investigating how adversity, specifically stress, affects the developing brain. To regulate stress, our bodies utilize the hypothalamic-pituitary-adrenal (HPA) axis. The HPA axis regulates how chemical signals transmit through the brain as our bodies react to stressful situations. When potential danger presents itself, the hypothalamus region of the brain releases a chemical that triggers receptors in the pituitary gland. The pituitary gland then releases signaling hormones that alert the adrenal glands. The adrenal glands produce stress hormones which awaken defense responses such as elevated heart rate, clammy skin, and fear and anxiety emotions. As an output, this results in high levels of cortisol, norepinephrine, and adrenaline in the body. This figure below provides a visual of the brain's stress response process.

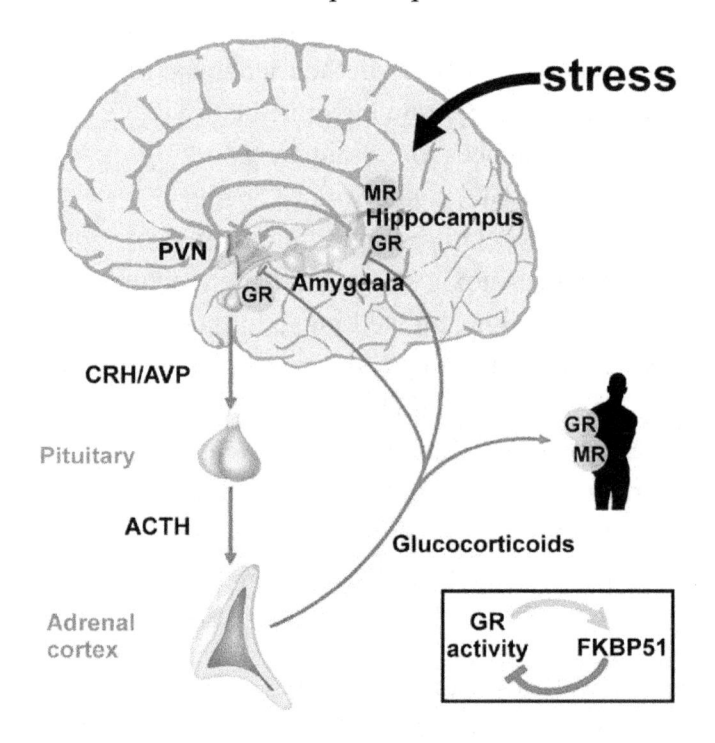

Figure 4.1 The Brain's Stress Response Process, *Frontiers in Psychiatry*, retrieved from ournal.frontiersin.org/article/10.3389/fpsyt.2013.00080/. 2013 Copyright by Raabe and Sprengler

Neurotransmitters also trigger increased glucose levels, prompting inflammatory proteins to race through the bloodstream (Tough, 2012). While these stress hormones are protective and essential for survival, excessively high levels can be toxic. Similar to other mammals, our stress response system is designed to react to brief acute stress. Mental stress overloads the HPA axis by requiring the body's response system to run over long periods of time rather than the brief emergencies it is designed to handle (Sapolsky, 1994).

In the early 1990s, neuroendocrinologist, Bruce McEwen defined the theory of *allostasis*- the "wear and tear" on the body due to the stress management system being overworked through prolonged stress. The body's process of coping and responding to stress, then eventually returning to homeostasis, is referred to as *allostatic load*, which is responsible for the eventual breakdown of the of the bodies stress management system. McEwen describes these destructive effects as observable. For example, elevated blood pressure provides increased blood flow, aiding muscles and organs in response to stressful situations (McEwen, Protection and Damage from Acute and Chronic Stress: Allostasis and Allostatic Overload and Relevance to the Pathophysiology of Psychiatric Disorders, 2004).

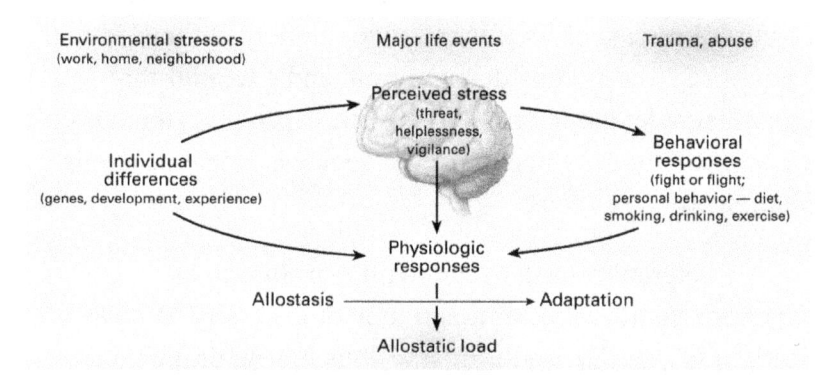

Figure 4.2 The Brain in Allostasis, *American Pycological Society,* retrieved from http://physrev.physiology.org/content/87/3/873. 1998 Copyright, Massachusetts Medical Society

The stress and adversity in my childhood must have been literally wreaking havoc inside my brain. I can only imagine how often my HPA was triggered and running at top speed for an excessive period of time. While physical evidence of stress from my childhood like blood pressure are not available, I can assume from environmental stressors, major life events, and instances of trauma/abuse that I would have experienced this allostatic load and begun the gradual breakdown of my stress management systems.

The National Scientific Council on the Developing Child has distinguished three levels of stress (figure 4.3) in children and adolescents: positive, tolerable, and toxic. Each level is characterized by to intensity and duration of stress response. A positive stress response is brief and moderate in magnitude. Positive stress is typically accompanied by a caring and responsive adult available to aide in coping with the stressor, resulting in a quick return to homeostasis. Positive stress, such as frustration, or anxiety associated with a new situation, is considered normal and essential for growth and development. Positive stress provides the body an opportunity to utilize the adaptive stress response and is biologically designed.

Tolerable stress occurs with exposure to an experience with a greater magnitude of adversity, such as death in the family, enduring a serious injury, or parental divorce. When buffered by supportive relationships with caring adults, tolerable stress provides a child the opportunity to learn to cope with stress. Prolonged or frequent activation of the bodies stress response system without the buffering of supportive adult relationships is considered toxic stress. The ACEs above describe toxic stress (Felitti, et al., 1998).

Positive
Brief increases in heart rate,
mild elevations in stress hormone levels.

Tolerable
Serious, temporary stress responses,
buffered by supportive relationships.

Toxic
Prolonged activation of stress response systems
in the absence of protective relationships.

Figure 4.3 Levels of Stress, *Harvard Center on the Developing Child,* retrieved from http://developingchild.harvard.edu/science/key-concepts/toxic-stress/. April, 2016

Clearly, with an ACE score of 9, I was exposed to massive toxic stress. While one of those events alone may have been tolerable stress, the various adverse experiences I was experiencing as a child from physical abuse to parental neglect all compiled to create a magnitude of stress far beyond tolerable. Even with secondary supportive adult relationships, my body's stress response could not return to homeostasis due to frequent and prolonged toxic stress.

As the original ACE study indicates, stress is not only unhealthy in the short term. The prolonged HPA response to ACEs disrupts brain circuitry during the developmental years of childhood. The prefrontal cortex is most affected by stress. Evidence from both animal and human studies show persistent elevated stress hormones disrupt the developing brain structure and function. Abundant glucocorticoid receptors are found in the amygdala, hippocampus, and prefrontal cortex (PFC). Stressful experiences have proven to alter the size of these areas of the brain and result in difficulties in learning, memory, and mood control, as well as other areas of executive functioning (McEwen, Protective and Damaging Effects of Stress Mediators: Central Role of the Brain, 2006). The images exemplify toxic stress's effects on brain architecture, specifically the neural connections.

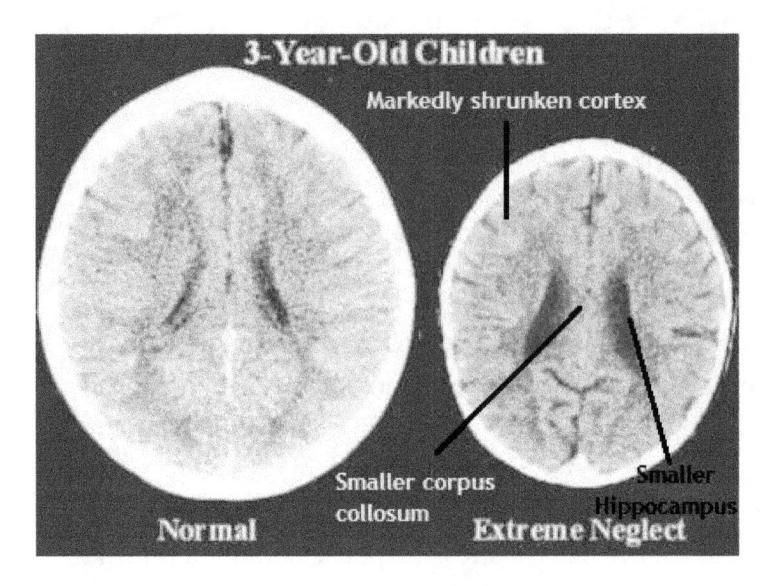

Figure 4.4 Childs' Brain after Neglect, *The Internet and Child Development*, https://childrenandtheinternet.wikispaces.com/School+Age+Child+Development.

Normal

Typical neuron—
many connections

Toxic stress

Damaged neuron—
fewer connections

Prefrontal Cortex and Hippocampus

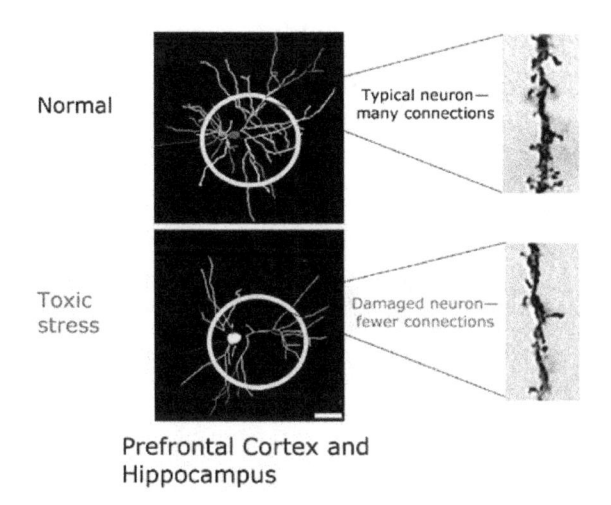

Figure 4.5 Persistent Stress Changes Brain Architecture, *Harvard Center on the Developing Child,*
http://developingchild.harvard.edu/resources/inbrief-science-of-ecd/,
Copyright Center on the Developing Child

Following their study on the impact of ACE on an urban pediatric population, Burke et. al (2011), reported that 3% of pediatric patients with an ACE score of 0 were identified as having learning or behavior problems in school, while 51% of patients with an ACE score of 4 or higher did. When science has proven high levels of toxic stress inhibit the prefrontal cortex of the brain, it becomes clear why children with high ACE scores have difficulty concentrating, sitting still, and following directions. A student simply cannot perform the functions deemed necessary to succeed in school. Chronic stress stimulates the adrenal glands to increase the release of cortisol and glucocorticoid receptors which send the brain into the stress loop shown below. As a result, the child will display a decrease in attention, perception, memory and learning capabilities, which inversely correlate with an increase of anxiety and fear.

chronic stress
- inadequate sleep
- poor nutrition
- emotional distress

increases glucocorticoids

decreased regulation of cortisol

↓ attention
↓ perception
↓ short-term memory
↓ learning
↓ word finding

cellular changes in the hippocampus

© Women's Health Network

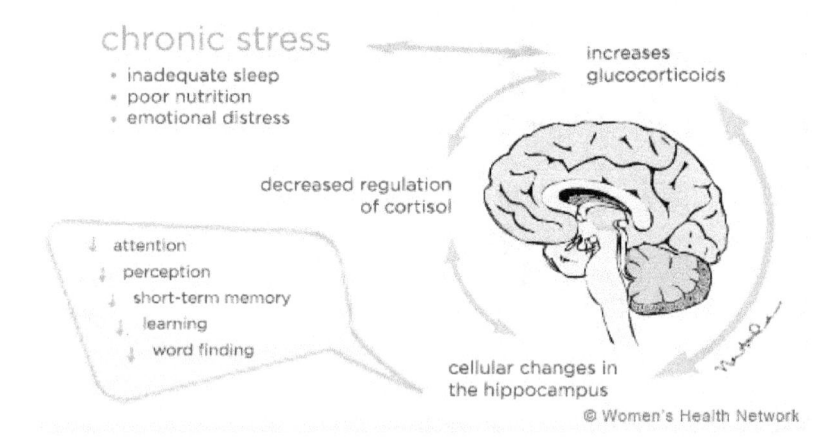

Figure 4.6 Stress Brain Loop, *Women's Health Network,* retrieved March, 2016 from http://www.womenshealthnetwork.com/adrenal-fatigue-and-stress/the-link-between-stress-and-forgetfulness.aspx.

While the hippocampus can turn off increased levels of cortisol, chronic stress hinders its ability to do so. This leads to an inability of contextual learning and the difficulty distinguishing between danger and safety in everyday situations: "Hence, altered brain architecture in response toxic stress in early childhood explains the strong association between early adverse experiences and subsequent problems in the development of linguistic, cognitive, and social-emotional skills, all of which are inextricably intertwined in the wiring of the developing brain" (Shonkoff, Garner, & The Committee on Psychosocial Aspects of the Child and Family Health, 2012, p. 236).

The prefrontal cortex, the area of the brain most affected by stress, also is responsible for turning off the cortisol response, as well as suppressing the amygdala which allows for adaptive responses to threatening or stressful experiences: "However, exposure to stress and elevated cortisol results in dramatic changed in the connectivity within the PFC, which limits its ability to inhibit the amygdale activity and, thereby, impair adaptive responses to stress" (Shonkoff, Garner, & The Committee on Psychosocial Aspects of the Child and Family Health, p. 236)

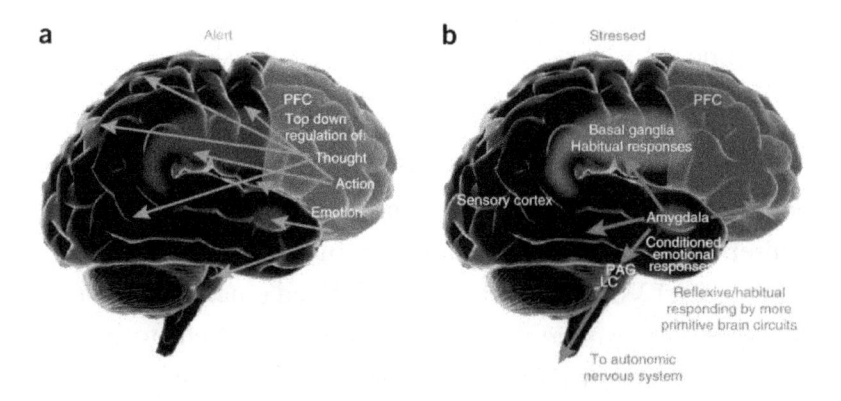

Figure 4.7 Alert Versus Stressed Brain, *Nature Neuroscience,* retrieved http://www.nature.com/neuro/journal/v18/n10/fig_tab/nn.4087_F1.html. 2015 Copyright Nature Neuroscience

The hippocampus and the PFC together regulate the amygdala's output of the stress response; however, when toxic stress exposure has altered the brain architecture and connectivity, variability in stress response can occur. As a result, some children may appear to over-react to mild adversity and be less capable of coping with positive stress. While the prefrontal cortex controls balance regulation of the amygdala, more importantly the PFC is responsible for the development of executive functions, such as decision making, working memory, self-regulation (emotional and cognitive), and impulse control, which I will explore further in Chapter Six.

In my life, trauma or ACEs converted to toxic stress, wearing on my body's stress response system. If you were to look inside my brain, very likely you would see damaged brain architecture similar to the diagrams. From the outside it may seem as though a child is resilient enough to overcome ACEs in childhood, but this research shows the how brain architecture is hindered during these critical years of development.

Post-traumatic stress disorder (PTSD) is commonly diagnosed in reaction to stress symptoms. However, PTSD does not capture all of the symptoms seen in traumatized children. Since the clinical diagnoses of trauma can be overly broad, Bessel Van der Kolk (2005) defined a new diagnosis *developmental trauma disorder* for children with histories of complex traumas, which attempts to span the emotional, behavioral, neurobiological, and developmental consequences of trauma.

When a parent is the source of violence, a child's sense of security, and safety can be compromised or destroyed, replaced instead by fear and anxiety (Janoff-Bulman, 1992). A parent's unpredictable or violent behavior can lead to difficulty forming personal attachments and may foster relationships that are based on fear and anxiety (Sroufe, 1997). Trauma expert and psychiatrist Judith Herman explains how children exposed to violence view the world as a threatening place, in which danger and hurt are to be expected:

> Adaptation to the climate of constant danger requires and state of constant alertness. Children in an abusive environment develop extraordinary abilities to scan for warning signs of attack. They become minutely attuned to their abusers' inner states. They learn to recognize subtle changes in facial expression, voice, and body language as signals of anger, sexual arousal, intoxication, and dissociation. This nonverbal communication becomes highly automatic and occurs for the most part outside of conscious awareness. Child victims learn to respond without being able to name or identify the danger signals that evoked their alarm (p. 99).

Therefore, students such as myself who are exposed to trauma are coming into the classroom in this constant state of alertness, also referred to as survival mode.

As my memoir reflects, I remember being scared almost all the time: scared of being hit, or yelled at, or hurt in some way. My childhood was, simply put, *really* scary. I always feared making a mistake because I anticipated harsh discipline. I never knew what would set off my mom, or her boyfriend. Indeed, it felt like walking on eggshells, constantly. While I lived in constant fear most of my childhood, as an adult, in retrospect, I am not sure if I find my environment most disturbing, or knowing the damage that occurred inside my brain. Every child's experience is vastly unique; however, the life-long results of these brain researchers have proven to be eerily apt comparisons for my experiences. It would seem that adverse childhood experiences do dramatically inhibit brain development. Though, as the rest of my memoir will describe, I survived this damage—after first suffering its worst consequences.

Chapter 5: Acting Out

I had the opportunity to go to Bible camp for the first time the summer after my fourth-grade year. It had been a long year, having to learn how to help my mom after her stroke the summer before, so I was excited to get away from my family for the week. The first few days of camp were fun. I met a lot of other kids, swam, made crafts, and sang a lot of songs. I loved the singing. But it didn't take long before the other kids started to notice the weirdness about me. I started to feel left out and lonely. I missed being home.

I decided that if I got into trouble, they might send me home. Defiant is the best way to describe how I acted. I yelled at the counselors and staff. I went into my cabin and lay in my bed. I refused to participate in any activities. Two of the counselors grabbed me, one on each arm, and escorted me to the director's cabin. I pulled and jerked and tried to run away. They tightened their grip. In the director's cabin, I sat and stared as she asked me questions. I refused to answer.

I sat there and thought about how much I hated my life. I wondered how God could let me feel this way. I was here at Bible camp, but God seemed so far away. Eventually, I broke down. I explained to the camp director that I felt like the kids weren't talking to me. I wanted to go home, but really, I didn't want to go home because things were bad there, too. In that moment I remembered my neighbor—how he was sad and took his life. I wanted my pain and sadness to go away. I wanted to die, and I told the director. She was nearly speechless. I think my case was over her head. I doubt very many camp kids go ballistic like I did. In a desperate attempt to help me, the camp director called the police, who came to get me from camp. It was the first time I ever rode in a squad car. They took me to a crisis center in a nearby town.

    I sat there in the crisis center for over an hour. I sat there and thought about my life. Why was I so weird? Why did I have so many problems? I didn't want to die, but I hurt so much. I wanted the pain to go away, forever. Finally, the staff came to talk to me. They asked me lots of questions. I talked to them for about an hour, and, after I promised to finish the week at camp with good behavior, the policemen took me back to camp. The girls in my cabin were really nice to me when I came back, but I could tell they were going out of their way to be nice. I could feel the tension when I walked into a room. I think they were scared of me, scared of what I might do to them, or to myself, if they weren't nice to me.

    By fifth grade I really hated my life. It was so stressful at home, and I always felt bad about myself. I continued to think about the day that I saw the neighbor hang from the deck. *Why did he take his own life? Does life get that bad?* I continued to ask the questions over and over in my mind. Fifth grade was when I seriously thought my life was bad enough to feel like ending it. I no longer just felt like I wanted to die; I really wanted to die. I wanted to be gone, forever. No more problems, no more hurt. No more sadness.

    I started acting out in school. I wanted to die. I told everyone I was feeling this way. I told the kids in school I wanted to end my life; I wanted to kill myself. I acted out in all sorts of ways. After school one day, I went home and I hung my jump rope in the rafters of our garage. When my mom came home, she called the police. I was in the garage, taking the rope down, when the squad car pulled into our driveway. The officer talked to my mom for a short time and then came over to me and told me to get in.

He was the nicest police officer I had ever met. He opened the front door on the passenger side. I was surprised that he let me get in the front of the car. We drove around our small little town several times. For a long while we were both silent. I started to cry. He asked me to tell him what was going on at home that made me feel so bad. I told him some things and pretty soon I was crying so hard I couldn't even talk.

He pulled the squad car into his own driveway. I waited in the car as he went into his house. I tried to calm down and get myself under control. I was crying so hard that my body was shaking, almost jerking. The officer came out with a box of tissue, and we drove around some more. He continued to listen, only asking questions every once in a while. He looked over at me and explained that he was going to have to take me back to the crisis center. I looked into his gentle eyes; they were glossy, reflecting my pain.

"I'm sorry," he said. "I have to take you there. They will help you."

This was my second time in the crisis center. I thought the staff would talk to me and send me home, but they didn't. They showed me to a room, pointed to a bed, and said I would be able to see the counselor in the morning. I was by far the youngest kid in the center. My roommate was a seventeen-year-old girl with long brown hair and bandages on her arms. I didn't talk to her much; she seemed cold and distant, unwilling to hold a conversation. I think she resented sharing a room with a young girl.

The room next to mine had two guys staying in it. One boy was seventeen and the other sixteen. The guys were pretty nice to me. For hours we took turns playing Duck Hunt and Mario on the Nintendo in the crisis center. One entire night was consumed by an eventful game of Monopoly. The guys teased me for being so young in the crisis center.

"Why does a little shit your age try committing suicide?" they asked. From then on, they called me "little shit." I didn't mind. I was glad they were nice to me. After feeling like no one cared or even really liked me much, I welcomed the teasing. It was not the nicest name, but the attention felt good. I liked being around older kids. I welcomed the teasing and the name calling from the older kids. I felt as though they were being nice to me. My self-esteem must have been through the floor.

The crisis center seemed like an okay place. There were plenty of games to play. I baked cookies and made a ton of crafts. There was a pay phone where we could make collect calls, which seemed like a cool thing to me. To get to the phone, we had to walk through the detox center where there were some really scary looking adults, mostly males. Every day I met with different counselors and answered hundreds of questions. I wasn't sure how being there was going to help me, but my parents said it would.

I was in the crisis center three times, because I declared so many times I wanted to die. The third time was nearly a repeat of the second visit. Most of the time, I just wanted so much for someone to love me, give me attention, and free me from all the bad feelings I carried. But part of me really did want to die. I hated my life and resented all the bad things that had happened to me and my family.

In time, I got very out of control in school. I was interrupting the learning environment for other students, so the principal said I couldn't come back. The county put me in foster care during the day. At night I went home to my family.

Things at home were rough. My mom was always stressed about money, and having to do things with one hand. She hit me and slapped me around. She liked to pull my long hair. We fought every day over something. Usually, it started in the morning. My alarm would go off, and I wouldn't hear it. Getting out of bed in the morning was so hard, and I was never sure why. "I didn't hear my alarm," I'd say. Mom swore at me or slapped me. After school, we argued over chores, or something else. I wished my mom would be more like my foster mom.

The foster home opened my eyes, even though I was only there during the day. High school girls lived there, with their own stories to tell. I soon realized if I didn't learn to control my behavior, in several years I could be living there full time, too. I am really thankful for that experience. To this day, my foster mom has been one of the most beneficial people in my life. She believed in me. She told me over and over I was not a bad kid; it was only my choices that were bad. She saw lifelong potential in me and encouraged me to have confidence in myself. I actually started to believe in myself. I really enjoyed being at the foster home, mostly because I didn't feel scared. The sadness that smothered me daily began to lift.

In time, the county worker found a day treatment program for me to attend. Each day I rode in a van for about forty minutes to get to school and then another forty minutes to get home. The day treatment program was like a very small school, usually with only four or five other kids in my classroom. Each of us had our own cubicle desk, with walls separating us from one another. We had one teacher and several aides. For the majority of the day, we worked quietly on our assignments. One hour each morning, we had a group therapy session. Once a week, we were able to participate in a fun activity of some sort, like going on a field trip, if we had good behavior for the week.

There were four levels of behavior to earn points for. Each day we started a new individual chart with six goals to meet. If we met each goal for each hour, we earned a point. If we earned all of our points for the week, we were on level one. Earning most of the points put us on level two. Earning only some points left us at level three. Earning almost no points demoted us to level four.

I worked hard most of the time to be on level one or two. The prizes were so rewarding, I wanted to be good and earn all my points. If I didn't earn enough points I'd move down to level 3 or 4, with very little privileges. Only once or twice when I had a really bad day, was I on level four. I didn't like being monitored closely. If I slipped even a little, points were taken away. It was frustrating, but for the most part I enjoyed going to school there. The best part was that there were older boys who rode in the van with me each day. I liked being around them. They made me feel older and more mature, they flirted with me. The attention felt nice.

I finished my fifth-grade year at day treatment. Because I did so well during sixth-grade, I was able to gradually work back into mainstream public school. It was a troublesome year. The friends I once had at school were cold and unfriendly to me. It was obvious I was a bad kid. Kids told me that their parents said they couldn't be friends with me anymore. It hurt. It burned. The rejection tortured me. I was filled with a deep sadness.

I thought maybe they were just being mean, but after school one day I went over to a friend's house to hang out for a few hours. Her mom was home. Her mom came in the living room to say hi. She saw me, chatted with me for a few minutes, and then told my friend to go with her into the kitchen. I heard her mom say, "She is not welcome in our home. I don't want you to hang out with her. She is a troublemaker." My friend came back in the room and told me to go home.

Like any other kid, I just wanted to fit in. The awkwardness of being a pre-teen was overwhelming enough, but I carried problems and now a label, too. I was known for being bossy and forcing others to do things my way. I struggled to belong, to fit in, to be liked. I made up lots of stories to try to get people to like me, but it never seemed to work. One day I was a superhero. The next day I was a princess. The more kids ignored me, the more I tried to manipulate them into being my friend. My social skills led to a vicious cycle.

In time, my mom recovered from her stroke enough to regain her driving abilities. On occasion, my mom, brother, and I went to visit my aunt and uncle nearly five hours away. I always enjoyed going for visits because my cousin was only a few months shy of being a year older than me. I enjoyed spending time with her, and didn't feel as rejected.

Growing up on a farm, I really loved animals—especially cats. On this particular visit, my cousin and I were in the barn playing with the cats. For whatever reason, we decided to put a lead rope on a cat. I think we were trying to get the cat to lead like a horse. The poor cat did not like this game. The more the cat pulled, the more I tried to get it to lead. Pretty soon the little cat was not responsive. I took the rope off and tried to help the cat revive, but it still didn't respond. We realized the cat had died. Without knowing it, I had killed the poor, innocent cat. I felt so bad; I had no idea the cat's neck could be so fragile in the lead rope. I never expected it would be so easy to hurt or kill another creature. It seems obvious now, but I was young and I wasn't thinking.

I started to panic. I knew that my family already thought I was a bad kid. I had been ostracized on so many occasions. Everyone knew I was the kid who had problems; therefore, I was a disgrace. I would be in big trouble for hurting this cat.

"What should we do?" I asked my cousin. This was an old-fashioned barn, with stalls over a gutter that carried the animals' waste around the barn clockwise in order to get rid of it.

"Put it in the gutter," she suggested. "When we clean the barn next time, it will go out with the poop and no one will see it." So, I put the cat in the gutter.

Later that afternoon, the cat was found and I was in big trouble. Although it seemed like a joint effort, I received a much heavier load of discipline. Of course, I was the bad kid. In any occasion where blame occurred, the finger most often was pointed at me. After all, I was bad, and easy to blame. I hated myself for what had happened. I wanted to die just like the cat had. I wanted to be lifeless like it. Peaceful in death.

I was rarely trusted as a kid. My aunts, uncles, and grandparents all looked down on me for being such a bad kid. When we had a family get-together, it always felt like people were watching me, making sure I wasn't causing trouble. I could see it in their eyes, the way they looked at me, searching me with their eyes. Their puckered lips and deep sighs declared the sound of judgment. My other cousins played games, but often didn't include me. They thought I was weird. I was. I was some kind of weird, bossy, fat, bad apple and troublemaker. Mostly I was just plain bad. They believed it, and I was beginning to believe it too.

I went back full time to public school for seventh grade, but things were not going well. I was always looking for ways to fit in at school and get people to like me. In addition to making up stories, I tried to "buy" friends. I thought if I had the name brand clothes, I could fit in; if I had money (which we didn't), things would be okay.

One time at my dad's house, I found a secret stash of cash. There was so much, I was sure no one would notice some missing. Eventually, when I got a job, I thought I could secretly put it back without anyone ever finding out. I pocketed nearly $1,700. Dad always had large amounts of cash on hand. I was sure he would never notice. The first thing I did was call up a friend and go on a shopping spree. I bought one of every name brand the store carried.

At school I had money! When I needed a favor like homework help or someone to open the door for me, I offered $5 or $10. I had tons of people around me. That is, until my mom realized that something was up and started investigating my room. She found all my new clothes and grilled me on where I got them, how I had money to purchase them. Some were still new with tags on them, so she made me return them. Eventually, she figured it out and I had to work off what I couldn't return.

Seventh grade was also when I started drinking and doing drugs. I snuck out at night and found older people or friends my age to drink with. Mostly we stole what alcohol we could get our hands on. We also stole cigarettes. It was a game to see who could be the best at stealing from the little local store. We soon found easy highs from sniffing rubber cement. We chewed Big Red gum to cover the smell. Soon enough, in my little group of friends who accepted me, I was on top of the world.

Cigarettes were in high demand at my age. It was cool to smoke. Young kids my age craved them. If you were brave enough to ask someone of age to buy them, or steal them yourself, you were popular among the young smokers. I so wanted to be popular in every way possible. Getting smokes was easy for me. I knew enough buyers, and I really didn't care if I got caught stealing them. I accrued cigs by the carton, and turned around to sell them. Marlboro Reds were everyone's favorite. Mediums were mine. I always had plenty on hand. A pack of smokes cost $2.13, so $2.25 was the norm, but $3 was what you gave the buyer to provide a small tip. If kids were underage and craved smokes, they could buy them from me for $5 a pack. I sold smokes like a dealer sold drugs. I took calls, met people in the park, arranged for drops. It sounds strange, but for a while I made a lot of money this way.

My mom has smoked my whole life. If I was ever desperate for a sale, I would sneak a pack or two from her. I could usually sell them to someone, but they didn't satisfy my own habit. My mom smoked nasty menthols. They were the cheapest off-brand you could find—*Style* or something like it. I tried them once. When I opened the pack, I could immediately smell the mint fresh scent. I took one out, lit it up, and inhaled. The rush of smoke traveled down my throat, the cool minty feeling crystallizing my esophagus and lungs. I started to cough. My lips were minty but my mouth tasted like smoke. Nasty. I couldn't get that cigarette extinguished fast enough! On occasion my mom accused me of smoking her cigarettes. Yeah, right! If I was dying for a smoke, I would rather have a big fat cigar than a menthol!

I discovered rubber cement, and it became my favorite drug. Near the beginning of my seventh-grade year, while sitting in art class, I recalled seeing something on TV about kids sniffing glue and getting high. What was it like to get high? In class we were working on a paper mobile. After cutting a few shapes of paper, I opened the jar of rubber cement and glued them down. I left the little cap and brush sitting on my desk, giving the jar freedom to waft fumes into the air. I felt a little dizzy and somewhat silly. As the teacher made her rounds to check on us, she stopped at my desk.

"Please put the cover on your glue when you are not using it," she said. I did as told, but when she left, I opened it again.

I wondered what it would be like to hold the jar under my nose and take long breaths, slowly inhaling, pulling the chemicals into my nasal path. At the end of class, while the rest of my classmates cleaned up, I walked over to the supply shelf and grabbed two full jars of glue. When no one was looking, I slid them deep inside my backpack. School was out in less than five minutes.

"Bonnie, what are you doing after school today?" a friend asked.

"I'm going home to work on an art project," I replied, winking and smiling slyly to signify that I had other intentions. "Want to come over?"

My place was perfect for private, after-school hangouts because my mom didn't get home until 5:15, which meant we had nearly two hours to ourselves. As soon as my friend and I made it to my house we dropped our backpacks by the door, grabbed the two bottles of glue, and headed to the basement to my room. I opened the little jar and set the cap and brush on my dresser. I rested the edge of the jar just above my upper lip and took a deep breath, took another deep breath, and inhaled deeply. The room started spinning. Noises and small voices seemed to get higher and higher, then trail off. My friend was talking to me but I couldn't make out what she was saying. I lay on my bed. This was high? Cool. I looked over at my friend.

"I'm cementing the floor," she said. She repeated it. It took me a few times to grasp what she was doing. I looked over and saw the pile of glue on my bedspread.

"What are you doing, you dork? Quit dumping it out," I said. I grabbed the little brush and tried to scoop the glue back into her jar. After wiping up most of it, I reached for my sock and pulled it off my foot.

"Here, wipe it up," I told her, tossing the sock to her. I put the cap on her jar and set it down. I looked for my jar, but could not find it. Where was it? The whole room was spinning. I felt like I was on a carnival ride that was out of control. I got on my knees and looked under my bed. There it was. I had set it under the edge of my bed. I looked inside. The glue was nearly gone. I stuck my finger inside. It was dry. Where had it gone? I knew I hadn't spilled it. I couldn't believe that entire jar of glue evaporated into fumes. Oh well. I threw it in the trash.

"Want to get high again tomorrow?" my friend asked me. I looked over at her, sprawled out next to the new yellow-brown stain on my bedspread. My head was so foggy. My vision was cloudy as my eyes struggled to focus.

"Sure, but it's your turn to get the glue," I told her.

On occasion, I actually tried to do the right thing. Once, when my little group of friends went on a shoplifting spree, I stole perfume and diet pills. It didn't take long before the guilt consumed me. My mom noticed and asked me, "What's wrong?" I told her I had stolen some things from a store. She listened patiently and together we came up with some options. Between my mom and me, we decided going back to the store to return the stolen merchandise and apologize in person was the best plan.

Mom took me to the store. I walked in and went to the service counter. I set the stolen items on the counter and told the cashier I needed to make a return.

"Do you have a receipt?" she asked.

"No," I said quietly. The lady proceeded to complete the return process.

"I'm not returning these," I said. "I mean, well, I am, but I didn't pay for them, so you can't give me money back." I tried to explain quietly without drawing attention to myself. The lady looked at me hard.

"I stole these, and I want to give them back," I said, hoping no one else heard. I was so embarrassed. I felt like such a criminal.

"What?" the cashier questioned.

I turned around, looking for my mom, who had insisted I do this on my own. I waved her over.

"Mom, she doesn't get it," I explained. My mom proceeded to tell the cashier the same things I had just said.

The cashier paged over the loudspeaker: "Manager to service counter, regarding stolen merchandise." *Excuse me while I fall over and die of embarrassment.* When the manager got to the counter, the cashier explained I was trying to return stolen goods. The conversation was loud and people were definitely starting to stare at me. The manager came over to talk to me and my mom. At first, he thought I was connected to some other kids who had just been busted for shoplifting, so he told my mom the police were on the way. *My stomach sank, I was scott-free and now I am getting arrested? Crap, why did I try to be honest?* Eventually the manager realized I had not been with the other kids and understood what we were trying to do. *I guess most people don't actually come clean and return stolen items. If guilt weren't a factor, I wouldn't have, either.*

"I'm sorry," I said. I handed the Dexatrim and perfume I had stolen earlier to the manager. He looked at me sternly and said, "Thank you, for doing the right thing."

Thank you, for not arresting me. Then it was over. Returning those items was mostly embarrassing, but unfortunately it didn't teach me not to shoplift. It taught me how to be better at hiding the guilt. I was officially becoming a bad person. I was on a downward spiral of bad choices; however, I couldn't see it at the time. Did it matter? Everyone thought I was bad anyway.

Dealing with the consequences of my frequent bad choices was stressful. My brother was an easy target for taking out my stress. Whenever he made me mad, I lost it, hitting him as hard as I could. I sat on top of him and slapped and choked him until I got scared that I might kill him. All of the anger and hurt inside me felt like it was dancing through my body and exploding out my fingertips, which were wrapped tightly around his neck. It was so easy to hurt him. He feared me. One time I asked him to do something for me and he refused, so I took out the biggest knife in the kitchen and chased him around the house. I never had any intentions of actually using it to hurt him. I just wanted to scare him. When the anger subsided, I felt bad for the way I treated my brother. I hated my life, and I was scared he would grow up to feel the same way. *Please God, give Bruce a better life than me.*

I was so out of control. The anger inside of me, arguing and fighting at home—usually over my behavior—was so intense. In the autumn of seventh grade, my mom picked me up after school. I got in the car and sat silently, practically holding my breath. I knew something was going on because my mom never picked me up after school.

"You will need to pack your bags tonight, because you are going away for a while," she told me in a very firm voice.

"Am I going to a foster home?" I asked. The memories of my last foster home ran through my mind. I was excited at the opportunity for a safe environment. I loved my foster mom and it would be awesome to live there.

"No. You are going somewhere else," Mom said even more sternly.

I was beyond foster homes. The county strongly encouraged my mom to send me away to a group home for girls. That night, I packed my bags. I had no idea where I was going or what to bring, but my mom told me to pack and I was going to be gone for a long time. The next morning, I put my bags in the car and I tried to come up with a way to change my mom's mind. I tried to be really nice. I tried to reason.

"I'm not changing my mind," she said.

After that, I didn't say much more. It took us nearly three hours to get there. We drove up to a big, three-story house. Next to it was a smaller house. *It doesn't look so bad. Maybe I will like living here.*

My mom checked me in. We had a brief meeting with the group home counselor and my social worker before Mom left. I was so angry with her; no way would I even say goodbye. The staff person responsible for checking me in led me down to the basement. She opened a closet on the far end of the room. Inside were about two dozen orange jumpsuits in multiple sizes.

"Pick a suit," I was told.

Next was the shower. The staff lady walked me to the other end of the basement and into a laundry room. At the end of the laundry room was a bathroom and next to it a large shower room.

"You will need to shower to get rid of any critters," the lady explained. "Here is special shampoo. Rub it in good to your scalp and pubic hair. Let me know when you have it on. I will watch the time. After twelve minutes, you can rinse."

I undressed in front of the lady and walked into the large tiled shower room. I counted six shower heads and a tub. I picked one, turned it on and rubbed the stinky critter shampoo in my hair. When I had it all over me, I turned off the water. The twelve-minute countdown began. I stood there in the big open shower room, naked, wet, and covered in shampoo that was tingling intensely. I was freezing cold. I started to shake. *How did I end up here? This is like prison.* The tears started to run down and drip off my face. I continued to shiver, my teeth clattering loudly. This was surely the longest twelve minutes ever.

After the shower, I put on my orange jump suit. The staff lady handed me blue booties with rubber strips on the bottom.

"You must have something on your feet at all times here," she informed me.

"I brought clothes, can't I wear them?" I asked.

"It will take at least three days to sort through your belongings. After that, it will depend on trust. If we think you will run away, you will continue to wear orange, so the police can easily spot you," she answered.

Run away? Now that's an idea, but where would I possibly go? Yeah, right. I can't run away.

The staff lady walked me throughout the house. She rattled off rules to me. I tried to listen, but I was trying to grasp all that was happening to me.

"You must ask permission to go up or down the stairs," she said. "You will be given a cleaning task every week. We call them details. You will do your detail two times per day and, if you have a kitchen detail, you will do it three times per day, once for each meal. You cannot go outside without a staff member. You must sign in and out when you do get to go out. You cannot go in the kitchen until you earn your clothes back. You will get up at 6:30 a.m. and be in bed at 9:30 p.m. As you earn more privileges, you can stay up later, watch some TV, and leave the grounds on a pass."

We walked from the basement with the showers, laundry, and TV area up to the main floor. Here I toured the kitchen, dining room (with seats for twenty-five), main office, conference room, and counselor offices. The stairs leading to the third floor were partnered with the most beautiful wooden handrail I had ever seen. It was old-fashioned, with wooden spindles on each step.

At the top of the second floor straight ahead was a large community bathroom with stalls similar to the girls' room at school. In addition to the large bathroom were six bedrooms, with fifteen beds total. Four of the rooms had two beds bunked; one room had two beds bunked and a single bed; and the largest room had four single beds. In the center of the third floor was another full staircase accompanied by a beautiful handrail that lead to the attic.

"Come downstairs and meet the other girls," the staff lady said.

All of the girls were older than me, some by a year or two, others by three or four years. A huge whiteboard hung in the dining room. Each girl had a section on the board that told her level, her points, and her detail. I soon learned that if you were new, you got assigned to kitchen detail—either dishes or cooking—as soon as you earned your street clothes back. Other details included cleaning bathrooms, hallways, the laundry room, dining room, etc.

Each week one girl was the detail checker. She was to go around and inspect every girl's detail. If a girl hadn't done a good enough job cleaning, the detail checker came to find her and she had to do her job over again. If a girl had to redo her detail three times in one week, she failed the detail, and the next week she was assigned the same detail again. I learned fast to do it right the first time.

We got points for completing our detail, but if we had to redo it, we lost our points. We also earned points for keeping our room clean, making our bed, and, of course, for having good behavior. When we had earned enough points, we could apply for a level. To apply, you created a contract, which every girl in the house signed, stating they agreed you were ready for the level. Then you had to memorize a certain number of the Twelve Steps and during group time recite your memory work and answer questions. If the counselor approved, you were granted the level.

I think I earned level one in less than a month. It took me forever to earn level two because more was expected of me for each ascending level. I would get really close and then I would do something stupid, say something dumb, or have a bad attitude about something, which caused me to lose points.

Nonetheless, at some point the director began trusting me. The group home was responsible for a paper route and one girl earned the privilege of doing it. The girl doing the paper route at that time went home, so the route was given to another girl. None of the older girls wanted the route, so it was shared between me and another girl. We took turns in the morning getting up and delivering the papers. I had a paper route of my own before I moved there, so I was familiar with how it worked.

On rare days, the two of us girls got to go together, although I liked going alone. It was forty minutes of cold Minnesota tranquility. It was complete freedom. Each morning I delivered the papers, I thought how easy it would be to run, but I never did. I appreciated the freedom and returned to the home. I knew if I messed up, I would be in a lot of trouble and the trust would be hard to earn back.

Once a week, we were taken into the community for free time fun activities. All of us piled in and out of two fifteen-passenger vans. The community saw us coming a mile away. If we had worn orange jumpsuits, we wouldn't be recognized any more than we were in our regular clothes. It was obvious we were from the group home. Each free time activity provided fun along with a certain level of public humiliation.

Some of the girls in the home were extremely tough. The scariest girls at the group home, to me, were the Native American girls from the reservations in northern Minnesota. They all seemed alike—quiet and mystical. The look in their eyes carried deep, dark secrets. Many wore homemade ink tattoos on their hands and face. I wasn't sure what it meant, but I had never seen anything like it before. I knew not to mess with them. This proved to be probably one of the best choices I made. At one point, I was assigned to a room with one of these girls. If I didn't talk to her, we were fine. One day for whatever reason—I looked at her wrong or something—she came running after me. I ran up the stairs as fast as I could and into our room. I slammed the bedroom door and held it shut with all of my weight against it. Outside the door, she continued to swear and say things in another language I couldn't understand. She tried to push the door open, making a small gap before the door closed quickly with all my body defending the back side. I was so relieved when the staff came to restrain her, but scared after that occurrence. I wasn't even sure what set her off, but I certainly didn't want to make that mistake again. I was very careful around the native girls at the group home. They were intimidating, and I didn't want to take any chances.

My dad came to visit me a few times. One time he was able to check me out of the home on a pass for a few hours to take me to the mall. I desperately needed to get personal items, so I was really glad he took me. Dad told me I could pick out anything I needed. I picked out the biggest container of laundry soap and grabbed shampoo, conditioner, and toothpaste. I stopped and stared longingly at the tampons. I really wanted to get a box. The group home only provided a stock of large, extra-absorbency sanitary pads with wings. They were the equivalent of menstrual diapers, and I hated them. To have tampons was a pure luxury. I so wanted to grab a box, but I was so embarrassed to have my dad pay for them. The embarrassment prevailed, and I went without.

Just after I celebrated my fourteenth birthday in the home, I was trusted enough to go to church. My dad was always asking if I was going to church and, since he was Catholic, I thought I should try that to make him happy. One of the staff members attended the local Catholic Church, so she picked me up on Sunday mornings. I wasn't so crazy about the Catholic Church, but I was free from the home for a short time each week, so it was worth it.

In the church bulletin I read: YOUTH GROUP MEETS WEDNESDAY NIGHT FOR HAYRIDE! It sounded fun. Somehow, I talked the staff into letting me go. I didn't know anyone, and I felt like such an outcast. The youth group obviously had their cliques, and I wasn't welcome. However, the freedom was amazing. I was able to be trusted to be away from the home, enjoy a fun activity, and eat lots of snacks.

About a month later, I attended a tech, which is a weekend retreat put on by the Catholic Church. While the group home let me go during the day, they made me come back at night to sleep. I wasn't allowed to stay over. The second day of the tech, I attended a workshop on pro-life. There was a familiar face and I remembered her from the group home. During the holiday season she had come in and painted beautiful holiday paintings on our windows. I went to talk to her after the workshop was over.

"Hi, my name is Bonnie," I said. "Do you remember me from the group home?" She nodded and gave me a big, gentle smile. I learned that she volunteered at the local Birthright, a non-profit organization for helping pregnant women. She was gentle and caring, and I knew I wanted to see her again.

One of the requirements at the group home was to complete twenty-four hours of community service. I heard of other girls working their hours at Birthright, so I asked if I could come and help my new friend Marilyn. My relationship with her grew. I liked her. She knew I was a resident at the group home, but she didn't care why I was there. She never asked and it didn't matter. She cared about me. She never looked at me like I was a bad kid. After I was able to move home, I still kept in touch, visiting her and staying with her family yearly. Her family was always excited to see me, delighted in my success, and never once treated me like a bad kid.

Along with community service at Birthright, I helped out at the soup kitchen. Usually I was able to go there with another girl or two. The soup kitchen was always an interesting experience. The other volunteers were nice to us. The people that came to eat, well, we just kept our distance.

Eventually, I earned enough trust to attend public school. After many months of being tutored in the group home, and several classes at the Alternative Learning Center,

I was ready to go back to regular school. I liked learning, completing assignments, and meeting friends.

In the end, I earned more privileges than most girls in the home. I was able to participate on the track team after school, which was a nearly unheard-of privilege. I did an extreme amount of begging and pleading for every privilege. Seven months had passed since I arrived at the group home when I received a phone call from my mom.

"Bonnie your cousin Sharon has passed," she said. "Your dad will be picking you up for the funeral." Mom was crying, and she didn't really say anything else. Later, the counselor shared with me that my cousin had shot herself. Then Sharon had been in the hospital on life support and doing well, but when the medical staff took her off the life support she had died. I was in a complete state of shock. I didn't know what to think.

In a day or so, my dad picked me up. This was my mom's niece and my parents had been divorced for many years, but I was glad that my dad came to get me and not my mom. The ride to the funeral was pretty quiet. Neither of us said much of anything. It was the worst funeral ever. My family really didn't talk to each other at all. Everyone was crying. My cousin Sharon had been only nineteen years old, only five years older than me. She was beautiful, smart, and outgoing. In the casket, she looked cold and unreal. It was hard to believe it was her.

My aunt didn't really say much to anyone that day, but I remember she said to me, "Don't ever do what she did. I don't think we can handle another day like this." I felt guilty in some way. I was always the one who wanted to die. I felt responsible for exposing the family to suicide. It was a solution for so long, and now my cousin took the out. I wished it were me, the bad kid, in that casket, not her. *Why does life get so hard one actually takes their own life?* Afterwards, my dad brought me back to the group home to finish my time.

About a year after arriving, I was released. It was the summer before I started eighth grade. I had been locked up with other girls sentenced for running away, grand theft auto, truancy, attempted murder, drug problems—you name it. Every other girl had a court sentence and answered to a probation officer. I was there because of family problems and even though I had never been to court, I felt like a criminal. I had done time. It was official; I was a "bad kid."

By now I had been in obvious major trouble at least twice, been expelled from school, and sent away. Everyone knew me as the bad kid. Bad Bonnie. No one trusted me. If my friends' parents thought I was a troublemaker before and wouldn't let their kids hang out with me, now what did they think? It was the worst feeling in the world. I was the first female juvenile delinquent in our small little town of five hundred people. Most knew my situation, and everyone thought I was bad. Even my family looked down on me. The invisible nametag I wore now read "**BAD**" in bold capital letters.

When I returned from the group home, I really wanted to prove to everyone that I wasn't a bad kid. Deep down I remembered what my foster mom had told me, "You are not a bad kid. It is your choices that are bad. If you have confidence in yourself, that's all that matters." I still had a small glimmer of hope that I could have goals, I could be something great, and do wonderful things with my life. I learned so many valuable tools in the group home about how to cope, setting boundaries with others, and dealing with confrontations. Even with my Bad Bonnie label, they had sent me home with the idea of a fresh start and a somewhat renewed sense of confidence.

Chapter 6: Assessment of Executive Function

The previous memoir chapter shows my struggle with executive functions, such as: decision making, working memory, self-regulation (emotional and cognitive), and impulse control. As discussed in chapter 4, ACEs and trauma can directly impact this aspect of brain development in the prefrontal cortex. In this chapter, I will take this further by analyzing the executive functions displayed in my own late childhood, as shared in the previous chapter. First, I will describe the levels and research of executive function and explore strategies for assessing difficulties in executive function. Then, I will apply those strategies in effort to analyze the executive skills that were displayed or lacking in the previous memoir chapter. Finally, I will revisit the connection between ACEs and executive function.

Executive function (EF) skills are a key component of neurobehavioral function. Masten (2012) defines EF as "a broad set of cognitive control processes that enable individuals to manage and direct their attention, thinking, and adaptations to meet adaptive goals" (pp. 375-375). EF skills develop and change over time with age and experience in conjunction with the development of the prefrontal cortex and neural connectors.

Executive function is a vast umbrella term for all the explicit cognitive processes that the brain is responsible for, as demonstrated in Figure 6.1 below, which shows a simple breakdown of executive functions. The term covers cognitive control process that enable individuals to manage and direct their attention, thinking, and actions to meet adaptive goals. Two terms within EF studies are "cool" and "hot". Cool EF is involved in tasks that require little emotional control and relatively abstract problem solving. Hot EF is needed for tasks that require control of emotional reactions or excitement, delay of gratification, or resisting temptation. School success depends on both aspects of EF (Masten A. S., 2012). In my situation, my cool EF skills were acceptable. I could complete academic tasks. It was my hot EF skills where most of my trouble existed.

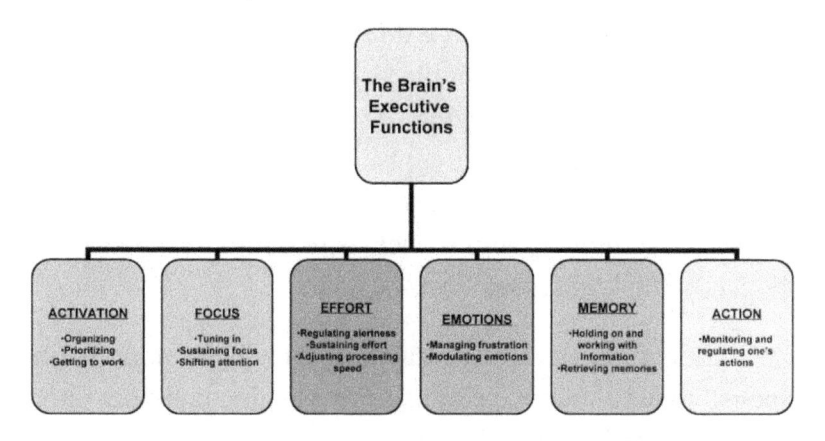

The Brain's Executive Functions					
ACTIVATION	**FOCUS**	**EFFORT**	**EMOTIONS**	**MEMORY**	**ACTION**
·Organizing ·Prioritizing ·Getting to work	·Tuning in ·Sustaining focus ·Shifting attention	·Regulating alertness ·Sustaining effort ·Adjusting processing speed	·Managing frustration ·Modulating emotions	·Holding on and working with Information ·Retrieving memories	·Monitoring and regulating one's actions

Figure 6.1 The Brain's Executive Functions, retrieved from https://cmschilly.com/tag/executive-function/. April, 2016

Masten also notes that EF skills are crucial for school success: "children must be able to concentrate, ignore distractions, attend to the teacher, follow classroom rules, get along with other children, wait for rewards, and suppress impulses to play, aggress, or otherwise expected behavior" (p. 376). My memoir depicts the difficulties I faced with behaving in school, and I believe my struggle was directly correlated to my lagging executive function skills. Self-regulation, especially, was lagging far behind and so controlling my responses was nearly impossible.

In the book *Assessment and Intervention for Executive Function Difficulties*, McCloskey, Perkins, and Van Divner (2009) attempt to bridge the gap between the interest in executive function (though they disregard cool and hot distinctions) and the practical applications by presenting the following definition:

Executive functions are directive capacities that are responsible for a person's ability to engage in purposeful, organized, strategic, self-regulated, goal-directed processing of perceptions, emotions, thoughts, and actions. As a collection of directive capacities, executive functions cue the use of other mental capacities such as reasoning, language, and visuospatial representation. (p. 15)

Essentially, executive function is the boss of the brain responsible for all mental and cognitive cueing and directing. McCloskey, Perkins, and Van Divner offer an extensive list of bulleted points regarding cueing and directing in their official definition, which can be summarized as the following: impulsive responses, interrupting, focus while screening distractions, cognitive flexibility, working memory, long-term memory, oral and written responses, regulating emotions, self-reflection, utilization of hindsight and foresight, generate inferences regarding another's perspective.

McCloskey, Perkins, and Van Divner draw attention to the fact that while there is increasing research surrounding executive function development, few attempts have been made to tie together the various strands of definitions, lists, and actual practice. Most definitions address the mental processes, including cueing and motor response, and pinpoint the prefrontal and cerebral cortex as the areas of the brain responsible for executive function. They developed the model in Figure 6.2 to aid in conceptualizing the interaction of various executive capacities and the prefrontal lobe function.

V. Trans-self Integration
Sense of source, Cosmic consciousness

IV. Self Generation
Mind-Body Integration, Sense of Spirit

III. Self Control:
Self Realization   Self Determination

| Self Awareness | Self Analysis | Goal Generation | Long-Term Foresight/Planning |

II. Self Control: Self Regulation

Perceive	Modulate	Sustain	Interrupt Stop	Foresee Plan (Short-Term)	Organize	Balance	Pace	Time	Monitor Check
Focus Select	Inhibit	Hold	Shift Flexible		Generate	Store	Execute (Behavior Syntax)		
Initiate	Gauge	Manipulate			Associate	Retrieve			Correct

Sensation/Perception Cognition Emotion Action

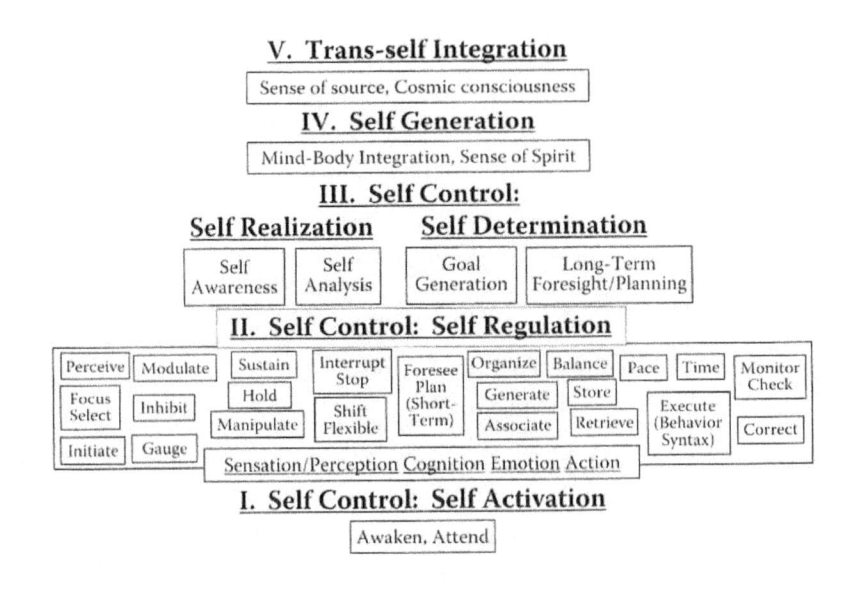

I. Self Control: Self Activation
Awaken, Attend

Figure 6.2 The McCloskey Model of Executive Function, Source: *Assessment of Executive Function, pg. 38,*   2009 Copyright McCloskey

The self-activation tier describes functions that cue the initiation of basic "core consciousness" related to an awakened state of mind. Self-activation typically relates to wakening in the morning, and getting out of bed. If you recall from the story, many of the daily arguments between my mother and I began in the morning, because I struggled to get out of bed. Self-activation relates to how our executive capacities awaken from sleep. Even though I would get 8 to 9 hours of sleep each night, it felt as though my brain was not fully working for at least an hour after waking up. Transition from unconsciousness to consciousness may involve a gradual ramping up of executive functions. This state is referred to as sleep inertia (McCloskey, Perkins, & Van Divner, 2009). While this may not be the absolute reasoning behind my difficulty to awaken and rise out of bed in the morning, I find it to offer a plausible explanation of why I resisted my mother, and why she could not understand my difficulty to awaken in the morning. In truth, even now as an adult, I have difficulty awaking in the morning and getting out of bed. It is a process of gradual consciousness, which I have learned to allow time for.

Self-control is split into three sub-categories: self-regulation, or functions that cue and direct behavior within the four domains of functioning: Perception, Emotion, Cognition, and Action; Self-realization, or functions that direct a person's engagement with activities related to self-reflection, self-analysis and gaining an understanding of personal strengths and weaknesses; and self-determination, or functions that direct a person's capacity for developing a personal set of goals and long-term plans that motivate and drive perception, emotion, cognition, and action.

In contrast to my difficulty with the self-activation tier, I feel I was and have always been good at the self-determination component of self-control executive functioning. Consider the example of how I developed the idea of selling cigarettes for income. Even as a young girl I had an inner drive towards goal generation, foresight, and creative long-term planning. Developmentally, my self-determination functioning was right on track, if not progressive, according to the diagram of development timeline in Figure 6.3, depicting the higher tiers of executive function.

Self-generation and trans-self-integration, according to McCloskey, Perkins, and Van Divner, are so advanced that they are expected to develop later in adolescence and early adulthood (See Figure 6.3). Self-generation describes functions that direct the posing of speculative questions related to ultimate source(s) and/or purposes of reality and physical existence, mind-body relationships, spirit, and soul; consideration of, and speculation about, the possibility of existence beyond the physical plane. Trans-self-integration encompasses functions that direct efforts to transcend conceptions of the ego-centered self in order to comprehend and experience ultimate source or an egoless state of "unity consciousness." The memoir selection in the previous chapter describes my late childhood and early adolescence. Therefore, executive functions relating to self-generation and trans-self-integration would not be expected at that time in my life.

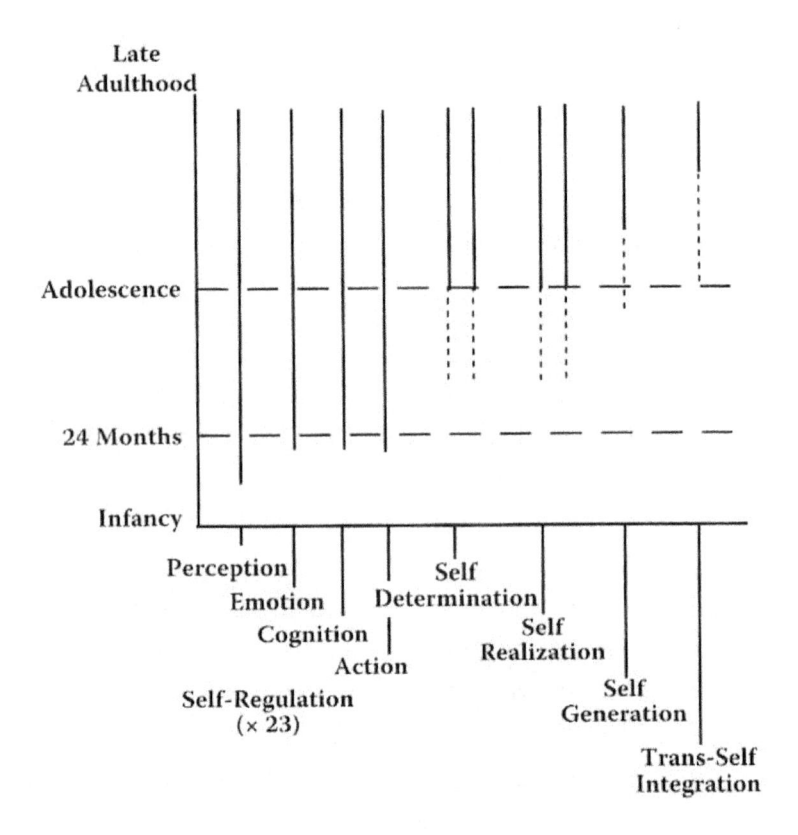

Figure 6.3 The McCloskey Model of Executive Function, Source: *Assessment of Executive Function,* 2009 Copyright McCloskey

Self-regulation functions are in many ways the most essential as they are involved almost every moment of our lives in all that we think, feel, perceive, and do. Self-realization and self-determination relate to self-reflection and intrinsic motivation. Self-regulation describes the largest tier, encompassing 23 executive functions responsible to varying degrees and combinations for cueing and directing functioning among the four domains of perception, emotion, cognition, and action. The majority of my behavior symptoms detailed in chapter 5 can be matched to categories within the large tier of self-regulation. Table 6.1 contains all 23 capacities outlined by McCloskey, Perkins, and Van Divner (2009), side by side for quick comparison. From these definitions, I delve deeper into my own self-regulation as compared to these 23 capacities through cross analyzing specific examples from the previous chapter.

Table 6.1
Self Regulation Descriptions

Function	Definition
Perceive	Cues the use of sensory and perception processes to take information in from the external environment or cues "inner awareness" for mentally tuning into perceptions, emotions, thoughts, or actions as they are represented "in the mind" or in the body.
Modulate	Cues the regulation of the amount and intensity of mental energy invested in perceiving, feeling, thinking, and acting.
Initiate	Cues the initial engagement of perceiving, feeling, thinking, or acting.
Gauge	Cues the identification of the demands (perceptual, emotional, mental, and physical) of a task or situation and cues the activation of the perceptions, emotions, thoughts, or actions needed to effectively engage the task or situation.
Focus/ Select	Cues the direction of attention to the most relevant aspects (perceptions, emotions, thoughts, and/or actions) of environments, situation, or contents while downgrading or ignoring the less relevant aspects.
Sustain	Cues sustained engagement of the processes involved in perceiving, feeling, thinking, or acting.
Stop/ Interrupt	Cues the sudden, immediate discontinuation of perceiving, feeling, thinking, or acting.
Inhibit	Cues resistance to, or suppression of, urges to perceive, feel, think, or act on first impulse.
Flexible/ Shift	Cues a change of focus or alteration of perceptions, emotions, thoughts or actions in reaction to what is occurring in the internal or external environments.
Hold	Cues activation of the cognitive processes required to maintain information in working memory and continues cueing these processes until the information is manipulated, stored, or acted on as desired.
Manipulate	Cues the use of working memory or other cognitive processes for the manipulation of information that is being held in mind or being accessed in the environment.

Organize	Cues the use of routines for sorting, sequencing, or otherwise arranging perceptions, feelings, thoughts, and/or actions, to enhance or improve the efficiency of experience, learning, or production.
Foresee/Plan (Short-term)	Cues the anticipation of conditions or events in the very near future, such as the consequences of one's own actions, or cues the engagement of the capacities required to identify a series of perception, feelings, thoughts, and/or actions, and the likely or desired outcome that would result from carrying them out in the very near future.
Associate	Cues the realization that associations need to be made between the current problem situation and past problem situations and cues the activation of the resources needed to carry out the required associative problem-solving routines.
Generate	Cues the realization that a novel solution is required for the current problem, and cues the activation of the resources needed to carry out the required novel problem-solving.
Balance	Cues the regulation of the trade-off between opposing processes or states (e.g., pattern vs. detail; speed vs. accuracy; humor vs. seriousness) to enhance or improve experiencing, learning, or production.
Store	Cues the movement of information about perceptions, feelings, thoughts and actions from the mental processing environment of the present moment into "storage" for possible retrieval at a later time.
Retrieve	Cues the activation of processes responsible for finding and retrieving previously stored information about perceptions, feelings, thoughts and actions. The more specific the demands or constraints placed on the retrieval processes, the greater the requirements for use of the Retrieve cue.
Pace	Cues the awareness and the regulation of the tempo at which perception, emotion, cognition, and action are experienced.
Time	Cues the monitoring of the passage of time (e.g., cueing the engagement of the mental functions that enable a person to have an internal sense of how long they have been perceiving, feeling, thinking, or acting) or cues the use of time estimation cues (e.g., cueing the engagement of mental functions that enable a person to have an internal sense of how long something will take to complete, or how much time is still left in a specific period of time).
Sequence/Execute	Cues the orchestration and engagement of the proper syntax of a series of perceptions, feelings, thoughts, and/or actions, especially in cases where automated routines are being accessed or are initially being developed.
Monitor	Cues the activation of appropriate routines for checking the accuracy of perceptions, emotions, thoughts, or actions.
Correct	Cues the use of appropriate routines for correcting errors of perception, emotion, thought, or action based on feedback from internal or external sources.

Before applying these self-regulation principles to my life, it is helpful to also consider the concept of arenas of involvement. In addition to the four domains of perception, cognition, emotion, and action, considering arenas of involvement offers a deeper dimension for critical understanding of the range of variability in self-regulation capacities. After all, executive function can vary depending on whether the individual is attempting to control ones internal state (interpersonal arena), interactions with others (interpersonal arena), interactions with their current environment (environmental area), or engaging with the culturally derived symbol system of processing and sharing information (symbol system arena) (McCloskey, Perkins, & Van Divner, 2009).

Comparing the Table 6.1 of definitions above and Table 6.2 of domains below, it becomes clearer that the majority of my individual executive difficulties centered on cueing and directing appropriate cognitive, emotional, and motor capacities in interpersonal relationships. Table 6.2 outlines the areas of self-regulation and the domain and the related arena of involvement, as defined by McClosky. This provides a quick and brief outline depicting the connection between definition and personal example.

Table 6.2

Personal Self-Regulation and Related Domain Assessment

Self-Assessment	Self-Regulation	Domain
-Unable to control temper	Modulate	Emotion, Action
-Dwelling, over focus	Stop/Interrupt	Cognition
-Misperceives others	Perceive	Perception
-Quickly offended	Inhibit	Emotional, Percep, Cog
- Poor listening to others	Sustain,Hold,Store,Manipulate	Em, Percep, Cog
-Unable to consider alternatives (own way)	Shift/Flexible	Em, Cog, Action
-Unaware of how actions affect others & anticipate consequences	Foresee/Plan	
-Hard to apologize	Correct/Execute	Emotion, Action
-Difficulty monitoring and regulation emotion	Perceive, Modulate	Percep, Em, Cog
-Acts without thinking	Inhibit	Action
-Poor planning, foresight of consequences	Foresee/Plan	
-Low ability read queues	Perceive, Focus/Select	Perception
-Shifting gears- transitioning	Interrupt/Stop/Flexible	
-Low ability to articulate	Generate, Associate	Cog, Action
-Unable to stop and alter actions	Interrupt, Stop, Shift	Action

    These definitions and arenas of self-regulation can be helpfully located within specific examples from my memoir as evidence that I suffered from lagging self-regulation function. Several of the above functions offer an explanation for my outbursts and temper. From a young age, my reputation preceded me. I struggled with controlling my temper and exhibited frequent extreme temper outbursts, both in the classroom and at home. This inability to control my temper relates to the Modulate function, where my brain was not able to effectively regulate the intensity of mental energy. I was unable to control myself and would curse and yell at anyone who tried to calm me down. I would not calm down easily, as it was nearly impossible for me to stop the outburst in numerous instances until I was physically spent. The inability to stop the outburst draws on the Stop/Interrupt function, meaning my brain was incapable of immediate discontinuation. Adult-initiated transitions were difficult for me, mostly because it wasn't my idea to shift gears. Transitioning stems from the Stop/Interrupt and Flexible/Shift functions in conjunction: the ability to stop what I am doing, and consider what another person is asking of me.

  Meanwhile, several other functions explain many of my problematic social experiences. Looking back, I now know that I often misperceived the actions and words of others that triggered my tendency to overreact. This problem derives from the Perceive function responsible for scanning the external environment and translating the information to inner perceptions. Additionally, my personality was intimidating. It was normal to boss friends and younger relatives around. I struggled to accept or even consider alternatives and went to great attempts to manipulate others into doing things my way. This relates to the Flexible/Shift function in the brain's ability to react to others' feelings and perceptions. I lacked consideration of others and often used threats of violence. Making violent threats exemplifies the Foresee/Plan functions because clearly, I was not considering the consequences which might come from making such serious threats. I struggled to apologize for my actions, thus relating to the Correct and Execute functions. In school I was especially disruptive, though academically I did quite well.

Even my own interior thoughts and mental health can be linked to several lagging self-regulation functions. Every day I had negative thoughts about myself: *I am bad, stupid, no one cares, everyone hates me.* I found myself dwelling on a range of things, from hurtful words which had been said to me, to scenes of abuse, and especially the suicide of my neighbor. Dwelling stems from the Stop/Interrupt function, in which my brain was incapable of discontinuing these thoughts and perceptions. I always felt a lack of control over happenings with my family, my emotions, and my thoughts. I was unable to control my impulses. I often acted without thinking, and most times it was to seek attention, which was usually in an inappropriate manner. This is an example of the Inhibit function, the ability, or inability in my case to resist and suppress urges.

Bottom line—I was smart, but emotionally out of control. Self-regulation seems obvious as the most prevalent of my executive function disparities. If each of the self-regulation areas were a circuit wire in my brain, some functions such as Store and Retrieve were working well. Others, like Interrupt/Stop and Flexible/Shift were not. Simply put, my brain was not wired to complete those functions.

Dr. Ross Green has developed the *Assessment of Lagging Skills and Unsolved Problems* (ALSUP) in working with explosive students. Note the similarities in the 23 capacities previously described in the self-regulation tier of McCloskey's model of executive function. While I find strong merit in McCloskey, Perkins, and Van Divner's assessment of executive function difficulties, I feel Greene's ALSUP may provide an easier assessment for educators and practitioners working with students in the classroom setting.

Using the ALSUP, I completed a self-assessment based on the previous chapter using a Lickert Scale, 0= never 1= sometimes, 2= often, 3= always. I then color coded my responses, creating a heat map (See Figure 6.4) which makes it easy to spot items of high difficulty.

Executive Function Lagging Skills	Self
1. Difficulty handling transitions, shifting from one mindset or task to another.	2
2. Difficulty doing things in a logical sequence or prescribed order.	1
3. Difficulty persisting on challenging or tedious tasks.	1
4. Poor sense of time.	2
5. Difficulty reflecting on multiple thoughts or ideas simultaneously.	1
6. Difficulty maintaining focus.	2
7. Difficulty considering the likely outcomes or consequences of actions (impulsive).	3
8. Difficulty considering a range of solutions to a problem.	3
9. Difficulty expressing concerns, needs, or thoughts in words.	2
10. Difficulty understanding what is being said.	1
11. Difficulty managing emotional response to frustration so as to think rationally.	3
12. Chronic irritability and/or anxiety significantly impede capacity for problem-solving or heighten frustration.	3
13. Difficulty seeing the "grays"/concrete, literal, black-and-white, thinking.	1
14. Difficulty deviating from rules, routine.	1
15. Difficulty handling unpredictability, ambiguity, uncertainty, novelty.	2
16. Difficulty shifting from original idea, plan, or solution.	3
17. Difficulty taking into account situational factors that would suggest the need to adjust a plan of action	2
18. Inflexible, inaccurate interpretations/cognitive distortions or biases (e.g., "Everyone's out to get me," "Nobody likes me," "You always blame me, "It's not fair," "I'm stupid")	3
19. Difficulty attending to or accurately interpreting social cues/poor perception of social nuances.	3
20. Difficulty starting conversations, entering groups, connecting with people/lacking other basic social skills.	2
21. Difficulty seeking attention in appropriate ways.	3
22. Difficulty appreciating how his/her behavior is affecting other people.	3
23. Difficulty empathizing with others, appreciating another person's perspective or point of view.	2
24. Difficulty appreciating how s/he is coming across or being perceived by others.	3

HOME- Problems	
1. Waking up/getting out of bed in the morning	3
2. Completing morning routine/getting ready for school	2
3. Sensory hypersensitivities	3
4. Starting or completing homework or a particular academic task	1
5. Food quantities/choices/preferences/timing	1
6. Time spent in front of a screen (TV, video games, computer)	1
7. Going to/getting ready for bed at night	1
8. Boredom	2
9. Sibling interactions	3
10. Cleaning room/completing household chores	1
11. Taking medicine	0
12. Riding in car/wearing seat belt	0
13. Other:	

SCHOOL- Problems	
1. Shifting from one specific task to another.	2
2. Getting started on/completing class assignments.	1
3. Interactions with a particular classmate/teacher.	2
4. Behavior in hallway/at recess/in cafeteria/on school bus/waiting in line.	2
5. Talking at appropriate times.	3
6. Academic tasks/demands, e.g., writing assignments.	0
7. Handling disappointment/losing at a game/not coming in first/not being first in line.	2

Figure 6.4. Self-Assessment of Lagging Skills

Standing on the body of research presented in this dissertation, it is highly likely the trauma in my childhood impacted the development of my prefrontal lobe, assuming the notion the executive function is indeed malleable. A possible intervention building on my executive function strengths and attempting to develop my difficulties would have been most appropriate. Clearly, my capacity for self-determination was far outpacing my development of self-regulation capacities. Looking back, it seems likely my profile pinned my issues to being interpreted as character flaws and/or the result of bad parenting and was on track to being labeled emotionally disturbed. According to Dr. Ross Greene, children who are most commonly referred for mental health assistance are paradoxically the most poorly understood. The behavior management systems of the day treatment program, and group home appeared to be working in replacing my negative or failing skills with more positive functions, but perhaps not for the reasons that they thought. I was not "emotionally disturbed" or full of flaws in the traditional, dismissive sense. I was not one of the criminals housed there. I was simply behind in developing these skills. In my own careful analysis after fact, I believe that I most often exhibited significant executive function difficulties in the interpersonal, and intra personal arenas. These then skewed my perceptions, feelings, and thoughts and actions that followed these miscues.

Children such as myself growing up in stressful environments have extreme difficulty with concentrating, sitting still, following directions, and rebounding from disappointments, all items which are required for success in school. When a child is distracted by negative feelings of diminished self-worth, and overwhelmed with uncontrollable impulses, learning, put simply, is merely impossible. This explains why, when a teacher asks a student with high ACEs to complete simple math equations or compile short sentences, there is a high probability the student may explode. Not necessarily because they don't like math or writing, but because their brain is not wired to complete the task. While many students who have high ACEs struggle with both hot (emotional control) and cool (academic) EF, in my situation, it was my hot EF skills that were of major concern.

By the time I started fifth grade, the main effect of stress overload on my prefrontal cortex resulted in the fact that I was having a hard time regulating my emotions. The trauma or adverse childhood experiences in my life had converted to toxic stress on my body's stress response system. Following the assumptions from chapter 4, my hippocampus and prefrontal cortex had been damaged, resulting in the output of lagging executive function skills. My behavior and frequent outburst were not viewed at as executive function deficits but rather defiance. I appeared to be a troubled young girl in need of discipline and consequences.

Through the context of brain development and executive function, a light is shed on the possibility that I was merely overwhelmed by uncontrollable impulsive and distracted by negative feelings. Clearly, I did not know how to manage my anger and had very little ability to calm myself down after a trigger or provocation. My world felt out of control, which explains my frequent desire to threaten or harm my younger brother or classmates, all in effort to *feel* in control. Lewis (1989) wrote: "Children try to overcome their feelings of vulnerability by inflicting violence on others" (p. 707). This situation is common when the child is exposed to extreme household violence. Exposure to violence can manifest in negative expectations and assumptions. Hopelessness, self-blame, and lack of control are typical feelings that result from trauma and may lead to overwhelming despair. When violence occurs at home, the usual protection and security offered by parents is destroyed and is replaced by fear and anxiety.

"I always felt scared..." Looking back, my exposure to violence explains why I always felt scared. Having been exposed to violence I lacked a sense of security. I had learned to anticipate constant danger. Judith Herman (1997) explains, "Adaptation to this climate of constant danger requires a state of alertness. Children in an abusive environment develop extraordinary ability to scan for warning signs of attack" (p. 99). This is what it means to be in "survival mode" and relates to the physiological stress response explained in Chapter Four. Children in survival mode cannot simply turn off the survival mode the brain is conditioned to apply. As you may recall the areas of the brain active in stressful states are different than those active in calm states, and predominantly the areas required in calm states are those needed for learning. In my situation, my brain had become very accustomed to survival mode. So, the learning activities I was being asked to do in calm mode were merely impossible and I exhibited explosive behaviors.

Research has increased tremendously in recent years concerning the role of executive functions in directing behavior (McCloskey, Perkins, & Van Divner, 2009). Recently researchers are taking a closer look at EF because it is proving to be quite malleable, even more so than direct cognitive skills. The prefrontal cortex is found to be more responsive to intervention than other areas of the brain, and stays flexible well into adolescence and early adulthood (Tough, 2012). Therefore, by focusing on strengthening a child's executive function deficits, we can increase the prospects for success in a practical and efficient way, which as a result promotes long-term resilience.

Chapter 7: Living Dual Lives

During eighth grade I got involved in every club and organization that I could. I went back to 4-H, joined Future Leaders of America (FLA), Peer Mentors, Knowledge Bowl, and Speech. I worked hard to stay on the honor roll, never the A because I am just not that smart, but I always tried for the B. Slowly I started to earn back some trust. I kept working hard, confident I could prove to be Good Bonnie.

Meanwhile, growing up in a small town there is not a lot for kids to do. I got bored. Before long I was drinking and smoking pot. Drinking was old news to me. Even as a little girl I took sips form my parents' drinks at parties and the bar. I liked drinking. I liked how it made me feel—except for the next morning. I drank beer and hard liquor, anything I could get my hands on. I continued to sell cigarettes for money.

Once, on our way to a movie, my cousin introduced me to some friends. We ditched the movie and drove around the lake. I watched from the backseat as the guy in the front passenger seat took out a pipe and a baggie and started packing the greens in the bowl. I had never smoked pot before, but I was curious. In school, I had heard about the side effects: memory loss, fatigue, depression. The effects didn't concern me too much, but I was really nervous. The guy lit the pipe with his lighter and passed it to the driver. The pipe was making its way around the car. It would soon be my turn. My hands were shaking. *Do I really want to do this? Yes. What if I don't do it right? What if I start coughing? I better take a small puff so I don't look like a dork.*

"Want a hit?" someone asked. I took the pipe. It was warm and it filled the backseat with a sweet, bitter aroma. I put my lips on the end, pulled the smoke into my mouth, and inhaled. I held it in for as long as I could, then slowly let the fainted cloud of smoke drift from my lungs. We continued to pass the pipe around the car. Several hits later, I felt calm and relaxed. Everything blurred. Before I knew it, I was laughing hysterically and craving junk food. I went home and put eye drops into my bloodshot eyes.

I grew to like smoking weed. Burdens were lifted as I relaxed and calmed my entire self. Smoking pot gave me an extreme sense of tranquility that I desired. I took any chance I could to smoke up. Anyone I could smoke with became a new friend.

I didn't want many people to know I smoked pot, though; Good Bonnie would never do drugs. Thus, began my split into two lives. Good Bonnie went to school and was on the right path. Bad Bonnie went to a lot of parties and hung around guys that were four, five, and six years older. I looked older and acted more mature than most kids my age. Some of the older crowd knew how young I was. Some didn't. Mostly no one cared.

Smoking pot opened the door to so many new faces who shared the same desire as Bad Bonnie. One in particular meant a lot to me. I met him at a party. I had already been stumbling around the bonfire, drunk for over an hour, flirting with guys and trying to determine who might be worth pursuing. I knew if I could land an older guy, I would be the envy of all the eighth-grade girls. There were many guys to choose from. I flirted with this one and that one.

Then one guy in particular caught my drunken blurred eye. He had blonde hair and the bluest eyes I had ever seen. I followed him into the house, leaving the bonfire behind. There were several people in the house. I found a comfy chair to sit in and admired him from afar. I watched as he talked to other people. I had to meet him. I stumbled over, threw my arms around his neck for balance and hung on. *If I don't remember anything else in the morning, I hope I remember him.*

"So, what's your name?" I asked.

"James. James McKee," he replied. I talked to him for a while. I don't remember much more about the night. I think I blacked out.

The next morning, I experienced a severe hangover. My head pounded and my stomach ached liked rotten emptiness. One thing was for sure—I remembered his name.

Most weekends I went looking for pot. I had several older cousins with connections. One cousin was pregnant and smoked me up (got me high) for helping her around the house. When her baby was born, I babysat and continued to help around the house. Her boyfriend was a small-time dealer and always had greens. Another cousin smoked me up for helping to clean and do dishes. I was young and didn't have a job, so I learned to trade services for smoke. One of the guys who visited my cousin wore a cool necklace with a secret: a skull head on a leather cord that held pot. He filled it with weed and told me that for a kiss, it was mine for a week. A kiss seemed easy for weed.

Every party I went to I hoped I would see James. I had remembered his name and now I wanted to know him. There was something intriguing about his light blonde hair and brilliant blue eyes. I hoped I would see him again when I was not as drunk. Maybe I could talk to him, get his number, ask him to hang out sometime. Of all the guys I was meeting, no one seemed as interesting as him.

In the phone book, there were several McKees, so I decided to pick one and call. My heart pounded hard in my chest as the phone rang.

"Hello," a voice said.

"Is James there?" I asked.

"No, you have the wrong McKee. Try Harold McKee. That's his dad."

"Okay. Thanks!" I said eagerly as I hung up. The words were golden to me. I looked in the phone book. Harold McKee. I found the number dialed, waiting nervously.

"Hello," a polite lady answered.

"Is James home?"

"No, he's at work, at Pizza Hut. Give him a call there," she said.

Once again, I cracked open the phone book. Pizza Hut. I dialed the number and asked for him.

I nervously asked him if he wanted to go out sometime, maybe see a movie. I held my breath and waited for his response. He agreed, and we made plans for Friday night. I attempted to ask my mom for permission to go on this date but was denied. So, I made plans to get a ride to the movie and go anyway. *Forrest Gump* was playing in the theater then. As James drove me home, we started talking about school. He attended school in a different town, so he had no idea how young I was. I was thirteen and in the eighth grade. He was seventeen and in his senior year. Four years doesn't seem like a big deal, except that a senior would never date an eighth grader.

"So, you're a junior, right?" he asked me. *He doesn't know? He thinks I'm a junior? I better agree or he will be really mad to learn the truth.*

"Yeah, I am," I sputtered out.

Lying was the easy part. Keeping it a secret was not so easy. We went on a second date. I wanted so badly to tell him, but I liked him so much and I knew he wouldn't go for it. I couldn't tell him, but soon enough people who knew me revealed my secret.

The dating was over, but somehow, we stayed friends. I chased him with the hope that someday we would date again and for whatever reason, he tolerated me and accepted me as a friend. People teased me for chasing him, but I didn't care. I always wanted to be around him; being around him meant drinking and smoking pot. I wanted so much to show him I could party with the older kids. So I did. This would prove to be another bad choice.

James played hockey. I tried to go to all of his home games. Getting rides to the arena, which was fifteen minutes from my house, was sometimes challenging. To see James, I often had to flirt with not-so-attractive guys to get a ride to the game. It was worth it to see him play. I grew to like hockey a lot. I thought it would be awesome to play on a girls' team. I did some checking and found a girls' team about twenty minutes away from my home that I could join. I had never played hockey before, but I was incredibly excited about the idea.

I asked my mom if I could play hockey. She thought I was nuts. She tried to say no but instead her answer was, "You can play hockey if you pay for your equipment." I knew plenty of ways I could make the money, but I made the choice to earn it in a positive way: not stealing it, not selling cigarettes. I asked my dad if I could help him on the farm, and he put me to work trapping pocket gophers. All summer long, I trapped pocket gophers on our farm and for the neighbors. I set fifteen traps a day on our old three-wheeler, "the cuss-mobile" (everyone seemed to cuss at it), and went to check them the next day. After finding a full trap, I cut off the gophers' front paws and saved the paws in a jar of alcohol. Each paw I turned in had a fifty-cent bounty, a dollar per gopher. I needed a lot of gophers, but it worked. It was just enough to buy used hockey equipment, and I was able to join the team. Playing hockey was one of the best things Good Bonnie ever did.

Good Bonnie was doing so well in school that at the end of eighth grade the school counselor told me about Post-Secondary Enrollment, saying, "If you keep your grades up, you can go to college your junior and senior year of high school and the credits will count for both high school and college. Best of all, it is completely FREE." Free college? No one in either my mom's or my dad's side of the family had ever gone to college after high school. Mom had a two-year accounting degree, but that was because after her stroke she had no choice but to go learn a new occupation. College had never even been discussed at home. It was tradition in my family to get a job after high school, mostly because there was no way anyone could afford college. I could choose to go to college? For two years? For *free*? I had to do it.

Suddenly, I had dreams and goals. I was given the ticket to do whatever I wanted in life. I knew if my first two years of college were free that somehow I could figure out how to pay for at least two more. I could go to college. I could choose to go college anywhere I wanted to go and become whomever I wanted to be. I was free! I spent the next year trying to figure out what I wanted to go to college for. An astronaut? Scientist? Doctor? Veterinarian? Teacher, maybe?

Around this time, I began confirmation class at my mom's church. It was a struggle. I was so eager to develop my faith and learn about God. I had so many questions, and I was excited to finally get some answers. I wanted to be part of the class, but I found it hard to control myself. I was often off task or made obnoxious comments. Nearly every week I was asked to leave class.

Bonfire parties were common. I could always count on a bunch of different people sitting around a big fire, getting drunk, and smoking pot. I don't remember much from one particular night except carrying around a bottle, drinking, drinking, drinking, hanging on guys, drinking, and trying my darndest to get to and from the bathroom without falling down or wetting my pants. I stumbled across the yard dragging my feet over every bump of the lumpy lawn. *I can't walk in a straight line, but I can't fall down because that is so uncool. I need to act older and be cool.*

At the end of the night, most of the people went into the house to crash. *Natural Born Killers* was in the VCR, and I lay on the floor and attempted to watch. I was so high and so drunk. I tried to make sense of the movie, but the changes from the color scenes to the black and white were too crazy. I passed out on the living room floor.

When I woke up the next morning, bodies of other people passed out were scattered all over the floor next to me. I didn't know most of the people, except I remembered kissing one of the guys the night before. I was pretty sure it was nothing more than a kiss. I walked into the kitchen and opened the fridge. It was my cousin's house, so I knew I could dig for food. Everyone was still asleep, but my stomach hurt so badly. *If I could just eat something, I might feel better.* In the freezer I found a bag of frozen strawberries. I took some out and tried to break through the frozen fruit with my teeth. I struggled through about six strawberries.

In about an hour, people started waking up and departing. My cousin and I decided to go to town to get McDonald's. I climbed in the backseat, allowing her friend to take shotgun. Two miles down the road, we each lit up a cig. I took a puff and inhaled. My stomach turned over and I threw my cig out the window.

"Oh, I feel so sick. Pull over! Pull over!" I yelled. I could feel the chunks coming. The car screeched to a halt. The passenger side door flew open and her friend hopped out, nearly rolling down the ditch. I didn't make it out of the backseat. The vomit came fast and hard. I barely had my head out of the car, but the stream made it into the ditch. The stream was hard and steady. Pieces of strawberry, burning with alcohol and chunks of stomach. I hurled three times. Wiped my mouth on my sleeve, sat back, and said. "Okay. Let's go." Up front they laughed about my panicked pleas to pull over and the remnants of strawberries.

I was feeling much better by the time we got to McDonald's. I was really excited to see that one of the guys I knew was working. He was gorgeous. I immediately started flirting with him. "Hi, Bob," I said. He gave me the most disgusted look. As we drove away, my cousin brought it to my attention that flirting with guys when you have vomit and strawberry chunks in your hair doesn't usually score a date. I looked down. I had vomit stains on my jeans, on my sleeve, and sure enough, chunks in my hair.

Meanwhile, Good Bonnie was dreaming about college, earning student of the month, and trying to hang out with friends who would never be caught dead drinking or doing drugs. *If I keep my lives separate, far enough away from each other, no one would know.*

Good Bonnie was almost caught being bad at school. I had been out the night before and I was extremely tired. No Doz seemed to be a good wake-me-up. So I decided to take two. Fifteen minutes later, I didn't feel anything so I took two more. Then two more, and two more, until the bottle was empty. Forty minutes later it hit me. I was shaking and jittering so bad. My hand refused to stay still and my head was spinning. I felt like a zombie stirring inside. I got up and walked out of class. My head felt like it was going to explode. My stomach was rotten. I went to the bathroom and locked myself in the stall. My friends told me later, they knew something was up and they were worried. They went to the office and said that I had taken something. When the school secretary came into to check on me I tried to lie and said I was fine. I think I passed out or blacked out or something because the next thing I knew I was talking to a doctor. I never took No Doz again.

Bad Bonnie kept making the choice to hang out with the wrong crowd, encouraged by having lot of friends, especially the guys. Eventually the guy I had met at the group home called me. *Ah ha! I knew I was better than the blonde roommate.* He only wanted to see me during the day, so I chose to skip school, and he came over to my house. Skipping school with Jake became a regular deal. Making out and watching movies was our thing. While we never slept together, we did everything else. I didn't feel like it was sex, because we didn't go all the way. "I'll smoke you up if you suck me," he said one day. I agreed, but was scared to do it. It reminded me of the silly games I had played when I was younger. I wanted the high, but I was so slow. I sat there and stared at his zipper and ran my fingers on the outside of his pants. I couldn't do it. I tried to tell myself not to be scared, but I couldn't push myself to open the zipper and reach inside.

He opened his pants for me. "I didn't take it out for air," he said. "Do you want help?" He reached for my hand, placing it inside his pants. I could feel his warm flannel boxers. He grabbed my head and pushed it down. *I really don't want to do this. Gross.* I closed my eyes and opened my mouth. I tried to do whatever he said. I started gagging, feeling the hot tears in my eyes, trying to think of something else, be somewhere else. I tried not to cry, I tried not to gag, and was thankful it was over. Our visits continued regularly. I hated giving him oral sex, but I liked the attention and I liked getting high.

The guys liked me. I wanted to be liked. So it became almost like a business for me. Exchanging oral sex for drugs and money wasn't a choice I liked to make, but I was willing to do it for the drugs. It was a just business decision. Getting high helped me to get rid of the tremendous pain I felt. Before long I became desperate for the high. I didn't care how I got it. Giving oral sex seemed repulsive, yet it fulfilled a habit that had more power than self-respect.

Summer before my freshman year was high time for sneak outs and smoke ups. Almost every night I went out and smoked up. Several times I went camping with my friends. Huddled in a small tent, we smoked for hours, getting completely power baked (really high). I got so stoned I forgot where I was and who I was with. Bad Bonnie always hung out with the older crowd. It was an easy choice. I fit in. I felt normal.

In ninth grade, the second year of confirmation, our class was split into pairs, and each pair met with an adult for our lesson. My class leader was also my confirmation mentor. I respected her because she thought I was a good kid. She was always happy to see me. *She thinks I am a good kid. She believes in me. I can tell by the way she takes an interest in me and wants to know how things are going.* Any other older lady asking me so many questions would have irritated me, and I would have judged them as nosy, but not her. She loved me, really loved me, and refused to see me as a troublemaker. "Don't you think I'm a bad kid?" I asked her.

"Why would I think that? You are not a bad kid," she replied.

Bad Bonnie hadn't been around for a while, but before long she was back at the parties. James had moved away to college, so things were different. I still craved the relaxing high that smoking pot provided. Getting to the parties was sometimes a challenge, but I knew the easy solution. If I flirted with guys who had cars, finding a ride came easy. Most guys I chased just to get a ride. I flirted for rides, booze, and pot. It was easy to manipulate guys to get what I wanted. Little did I know this would affect my self-image in the long run.

New Year's Eve, party night, there would be guys, and there would be pot. I hoped James would be there, but he wasn't. For the first time, I ate a funny brownie, made from cooking pot in the brownie batter. It was good. It was so good I could have eaten everyone in the whole pan, a million pans. It was a new kind of high and I liked it. Hawthorne was there, and I spent most of the night making out with him in his room.

I was so hung over the next morning. Still, Good Bonnie was going to work at the skating rink warming house in town. It was my first real job. Two other kids in town and I took turns managing the ice rink and warming house. My duties included unlocking the door, shoveling the ice and playing hockey with the neighborhood kids. I loved it because I could skate almost every day.

At school I chose to apply for a full scholarship to attend college summer programs. For two full weeks I was able to attend the theatre program at Gustavus Adolphus College in Minnesota, about ninety miles from home. It was a dream come true. My mom dropped me off there, but I needed a ride home and I knew Hawthorne would never come and get me. However, James was home from college and I knew he would totally be up for the road trip. I talked James and his friend Shaq (nicknamed for being well over 6 feet tall) into picking me up when the two weeks were over. The summer staff was cool and they let us have college privileges, meaning we could smoke if we wanted to. It was a great freedom. I liked the college feel and I couldn't wait to actually go to college. All I had to do was keep my grades up.

I tripped on acid for the first time when James and Shaq and some other guy picked me up. Shaq handed me a small piece of paper and told me to put it on my tongue. Everything seemed to spin. Colors stood out and became brighter. We went over to my friend Jackie's house and swam in her pool. The water felt amazing, but I kept thinking we were in a bath of oil. I felt like the world stopped and I was in a cartoon world.

I met some new friends that summer, older guys I had never hung out with before. Jackie had been dating one of the guys. Most of my friends had been bragging about losing their virginity. I felt like I was falling behind. I had made out a lot, but I had never had intercourse. I was dreaming of the day that I could share that with James.

Jackie and I snuck out and went to a party with her new friends. I had a lot to drink and began carrying around beer in "my fridge," which was a bag of ice that I stuffed beer into so I didn't need to go to the fridge to get one. We snuck back in that night and I was so drunk I almost woke up my mom and blew it. I felt invincible, so I put on a disguise and told my friend we couldn't be seen if I had my disguise on.

We chose to party with these new friends a few more times. I started to like one of the guys. Then one night I got completely trashed. The oldest guy, who was thirteen years older than me, told me to crash in his room. I was glad he was being so cool to me. His room had trash and dirty clothes all over the floor, It was disgusting, but I needed to lie down. He came in and lay by me. He started kissing me. I didn't want him to, but I was too drunk to tell him to stop. He pulled off my pants. I told him I wasn't ready, but he kept going. I was so scared. I didn't say anything. I just lay there.

I started to cry. He had his nipples pierced and they were scratching my chest. As he kept going, he started to sweat. The sweat dripped off him and in my face. I felt the drips in my ears, in my nose, and I could taste the bitterness in my mouth. The drops landed in my eyes and my eyes burned. I closed my eyes but the tears still ran. I never imagined my first time would be like this. I didn't say a word I was so scared. He finally left and I went home. I kept thinking: *Did he rape me? Well, I didn't say exactly say no, I was too scared to say anything.* I was so scared, and even more so I was incredibly embarrassed, ashamed, and guilty. I just knew I had done something wrong.

    I was excited to start tenth grade. One of the first things I did was get tickets to a big concert. Kat, James, and Shaq and I were scheduled to go. At the last minute, Shaq backed out so James swapped in a different friend, Jimbo. Jimbo was weird. I could tell he was on something, but I wasn't sure what. After the concert, we went back to James's place. Everyone, except for me and Kat, kept going back to James's room and finally I followed them back there to see what was up. They were doing lines. I had never tried coke before and I wasn't sure if I wanted to. I tried staying awake all night without it. The guys wanted to stay up all night playing cards. I tried to keep up with them, but I couldn't. I knew I needed to get some sleep.

    Bad Bonnie could hardly keep up with Good Bonnie's schedule and goals and before long I made the choice to do uppers to buy extra time in the day. I knew the first semester of tenth grade I had to make the top twenty out of one hundred in my class in order to go to college the next year. I was number twenty-three in the start of the year, which meant I had to make a choice to work hard and get some seriously good grades. Every minute I wasn't at work or attending a club meeting for one of my many organizations, I was studying. I studied for tests at lunch and even while walking down the hall to class I had my book open. In January, my report card came. For the first time ever, Good Bonnie had made the A honor roll.

For my sweet sixteenth birthday, I threw a big party. Bad Bonnie's friend's pitched in and bought me a pot pipe for my birthday. It was purple and silver with two removable chambers. As soon as I took it out of the wrapping, we packed the bowl and broke it in. I made the mistake of choosing to invite Good Bonnie's friends to Bad Bonnie's party. About then is when I remember things started to get messy. The two lives that I had tried so hard to keep separate were starting to blend. People who knew me as Good Bonnie were starting to see Bad Bonnie. But I just kept on. I had pulled the grades and I was going to college the next year; nothing else really mattered anymore.

Good Bonnie was working hard and earning money. So, in tenth grade, I decided to buy a car. Owning a car was not as fun as it sounded. I had to work a lot of hours to pay the car payments and the car insurance. In addition to all the hours I worked, I still needed to study. At a party one night I was freaking out about staying up all night and not having time to study. Stan, known for always having dope, was at the party.

"Let's do a line. Then you will be awake to do your homework," Stan said. It seemed like a golden plan. I wanted to be with James when I did coke for the first time. James was safe and I knew he could take care of me if something went wrong. Stan was convincing, and I needed it now. The first time I ever did coke, I loved it. I was sure I could run a marathon. I was hooked instantly. I liked coke, but it was expensive, so I only did it a few times a month. Before long, Shaq introduced me to crank. I had asked him to hook me up with a small line, a bump. Shaq didn't have coke; instead he had crank.

"Crank is cheaper, it lasts longer, and it's easier to get," he said. "I think I like it more just because it lasts longer so you don't have to do as much." We did a line of crank. It burned a little more than coke, but otherwise it didn't seem much different. I worried less about working so much, managing all the long hours to study after work. Crank made me feel super human.

I don't know when I started hanging out with Stan. Kat and I called him Freaky Stain. He always had a large supply of drugs. I hung out with him because I knew I could get whatever I wanted, when I wanted it. Most of the time he gave me the stuff without asking for anything in return. He suggested sex, but failed to make me follow through. When he wasn't around, I hung out with his brother Lyle. Between the two of them, I always had stuff. I chose to hang out with them nearly every night.

I went over to their house and they asked me if I wanted to drop acid. I had done it before, so I thought, "Why not?" Stain handed me another small piece of paper and I put it on my tongue. I didn't feel anything for the longest time. We started to watch the movie *Trainspotting*. The part where the guy dives in the toilet after the heroin and the part where the baby crawls across the ceiling totally freaked me out.

When the movie was over, Freaky Stain shut off the TV, grabbed my hand, and led me to his room. Everything seemed squishy, like I was in a bubble. We went to his room and I lay on his bed. He came in, turned on a black light and Led Zeppelin, and lay in bed by me. He started kissing me, and I asked him to stop.

"I gave you the hit. Now it's your turn," he told me with a big grin that seemed to vibrate off his face.

I finally talked him into bringing me home and just before dawn I snuck back in the same window I had snuck out of, beating my mom's alarm clock by mere minutes. Kat had stayed over the night before and she was sleeping in my bed. I jumped on her and woke her up. Still in a bubble.

"Time to get ready for school," I kept saying.

"What are you on? Your eyes look really funny," she said.

"They do? I better wear shades. Future's so bright I gotta wear shades," I started singing. We got ready for school and just before we walked out the door, I grabbed about a dozen Oreo cookies and hopped in my mom's car. My mom was furious that I was eating so many cookies, and she yelled at me the whole way to school. I laughed the entire time, which made her angrier. I never went to school high before. I thought the acid would wear off before school, but I was still in my bubble. I tried to act normal for class. I couldn't let anyone see Bad Bonnie.

Second hour, I took an algebra test. I couldn't get my calculator to work. I pushed the buttons over and over again, but the calculator laughed at me like a video game that I was losing poorly on. The next day I got my test back. I earned two points. One for putting my name on the top, the other for attempting to show my work, which looked a lot like a toddler had practiced writing numbers on my paper. I was pretty ashamed; I had really messed up. This was devastating to Good Bonnie. *All I had to do was keep my grades up.*

Good Bonnie went to school, then to work. Bad Bonnie did a line or two and then stayed up all night doing homework. Back to school, and then work. It was a habit. I was failing algebra and required the assistance of a tutor.

I kept hanging out with Freaky Stain and his brother Lyle. Instead of doing lines, we started smoking the rocks on a piece of aluminum foil. They called it "doing a foily." The foil was lit underneath with a lighter and as the rock melted you inhaled the fumes. It gave me a rush and kept me awake. I didn't like the bitter taste of the fumes. I preferred doing a line.

"We have to switch it up to give the cartilage in our nose a break," Freaky Stain tried to explain to me. *Whatever, I just want to get high.*

By the end of tenth grade sneaking out was no longer a factor. Either I went out after work or I walked out the door. Crawling out my window was a thing of the past.

Kat was my best friend. We grew up together, but the deeper into drugs I got, the further we grew apart. We are still friends and I love her, but things are different now. I had different priorities back then and my choices were hard for her to deal with.

Study time again. Another long night at work and still homework to finish. I pushed my books aside, making a clear spot on my desk. I reached over to my drawer and pulled out my picture frame of Kat, James, Shaq, and me at Valleyfair. It was my famous picture frame. I used the glass that held our picture inside as a plate. I picked up my blade. I walked over to my secret hiding place and reached my fingers in. I felt the sticky little baggy that held my rock in containment. I pulled it out, walked over to my desk chair, and sat down.

I put the little rock on the glass that protected the picture of me and my three best friends. I took my razor blade and sliced the rock in half, again, again. I continued to chop until the rock was broken into tiny particles. With the edge of the blade, I pulled in one side, then the other side, forming it into a line. Beneath the glass, I made the white powder line stretch from my nose running under each of my friends – Kat, James, and Shaq. The line curved up slightly because Shaq was way taller than the rest of us.

I carefully licked the razor blade and set it down. The tangy taste remained on my tongue. I liked the taste. I had grown used to it. It was distinct, a cross between a bitter-sweet tart and a fizz candy. I set the blade down and reached for my long, plastic fabricated straw. It was once a pen used to write answers on my homework, now hollow and used only to carry the sweet powder from the glass to my nose. I took a few deep breaths. I put one end of the former pen shaft in my nostril. I plugged the other nostril with my index finger. Inhale, exhale, inhale, exhale all the air in my lungs through my mouth far enough from the plate to not disturb the line I so carefully stretched out. I bring the other end of the straw to the beginning of the line.

All at once, I breathe in strong and hard, desperately pulling every particle through the narrow tube into my nose and straight to my brain. I let the tube follow the little line all the way to the end. I go back over the bareness of the glass searching for any remains while inhaling each lost particle. Ah, it stings. Stings. Stings. The tears swell in the corner of my eyes. I drop the straw. I take a few more deep pulls of air through my nose. Part of the bitter clump drops down my esophagus and rests in my stomach. The rest sits in my nasal cavity and slowly drips on the back of my throat. My eyes continue to water. Immediately I feel the rush, as if every single cell in my body begins to awaken. I feel my eyes peel wide open. I am energized, ready to run, jump every hurdle, turn around, and go back over the hurdles again. Awake. I'm wide awake and ready to study. My hands shake as I write in the answers on my homework assignments.

When the study session is over, I creep up the basement stairs. It is early in the morning. I am ready to sleep but wide awake. I want to come down. I want to sleep. I know I must get some rest because I don't have another rock to get through the day awake. I must sleep. The fastest way to come down is to eat. Quietly, slowly, I pull open the fridge. The bright light blinds me. My eyes adjust, and I scan the few food items inside. I am not hungry. I have no appetite. The thought of eating disgusts me. I must eat, it will make me tired and I can get some sleep before school. Nothing looks good. I close the fridge. On the counter I see fresh bananas. Repulsive. However, I must eat something. I think I can get one down. Just a few quick bites.

I peel back the sides and take a bite. Yuck. It is horrible. I don't want to eat it. My mouth is dry and my whole body screams *no*. I take another bite. I don't want it, but I know I must finish it. I take another bite, trying to eat it fast and get it over with. Keep going. I take another bite. I start to gag. My throat says no. I get a drink of water and take another bite. I have to eat this. Finally, I finish and throw the peel in the trash. I did it. I ate the ridiculous banana, and now I can go to bed. I lie wide awake until my stomach processes its contents and slowly the drug wears off. I become sleepy. Sleepy. I'm out.

I went on like that for months. I had to work full-time to pay for my car and insurance. I had to study hard to keep my grades up to make it to college the next year. Remember, *free* college. Last, I still had a lot of responsibility at home – chores to keep the house clean and help my brother.

All I needed to do was keep my grades up for sophomore year, and I could go to college the next year. Three months left of school and I had had enough of working late, doing the homework, and doing drugs to try to stay awake. I couldn't keep up with it anymore. I couldn't hold everything together anymore.

I was tired of getting up in the morning. After closing at Subway each night, getting up in the morning was really hard. I was pretty sick of going to school, dealing with the cliques, and my attendance was getting shaky. I went into school, cleaned out my locker, and carried all my books to the counselor's office.

"What are you doing, Bonnie?" he asked.

"I'm quitting," I told him. "I'm sick of this crap, and I'm dropping out. Here are my books. I can't do this. I quit."

"You quit what?" he said.

"I quit school," I said. "I can't do all this anymore; I'm done."

"Bonnie Laabs, you have three months left of tenth grade and then you are set to go to college full-time next fall. Why would you quit now? Are you out of your mind?" It's a good thing he didn't ask me if I was on drugs, not sure how I would have answered.

"I can't take it anymore; I want out," I said. "I can't keep working my job and doing the homework and coming to school. I need to keep the job to pay my bills, so school will have to go."

"How about I put you on independent study for the last three months?" he asked. "Then you can come in each day, get your assignments, and do them at home. How does that sound?"

"Manageable," I said.

So every teacher except one agreed to let me do my work independently. The Spanish teacher wouldn't budge. So each day I slept in, got up, did my homework, went to school in the afternoon, turned in completed work, picked up new assignments, and attended seventh hour Spanish class. After school I went to work, came home, and crashed. Because I could sleep in, I didn't need to do lines to stay awake to study. It worked, and I completed tenth grade.

I wanted to go to church, but I grew to hate church. I needed it, but every time I walked in the door, I could feel the judgmental eyes fall upon me, following me. I saw the cliques in church. I was an outcast to them, a disgrace. Why bother getting out of bed on Sunday morning?

Finally, summer! I picked up another job, bringing me to two regular jobs and a pick-up job. Most days I worked a shift at Pizza Hut, changed uniforms in the car, worked a shift at Subway, and then put in a few hours pressure-washing pigpens. Whatever the combination, I worked a lot. I worked a ton of hours and then partied at night. I got back into the bad habit of doing crank to stay awake. In fact, I would do meth about four to five nights out of seven and then crash.

I could go a long time without sleeping. I went to work high and tweaked out many times without thinking much about it. Tweaked is when you stay awake for several days at a time. By the end of the summer, I started having more severe problems with my stomach. It hurt when it was empty. It hurt when I ate. It always hurt. I was thin and my hair fell out a lot. I wasn't tiny, but for my size I was pretty small. I liked fitting into smaller clothes. The sad thing was, I fit because I wasn't eating. I was losing weight and muscle. My choices were really taking a toll on my body.

Good Bonnie kept on giving speeches in FLA and 4-H and working full-time. I tried so hard to be good and happy and make good choices, but I was drowning in pain. I felt guilty and ashamed all the time. I wanted to be a better person, but I didn't know how. *Nobody can help me. No one understands. I am in this alone.*

The rest of the summer I continued working three jobs and still seeing boys on the side. I had to work. I needed the money for bills, car insurance, and car loans. Plus my mom asked me to buy my personal supplies. Sometimes I didn't have the money, so the choice was often to steal the supplies. I relied on Planned Parenthood, so I did not get pregnant. Having a baby would ruin my college dream for sure. I rarely saw my dad. He worked long hours between his regular job and the farm chores. Besides, I was sure he didn't want to see me the way I was anyway.

I didn't eat much because I was rarely hungry- unless I wanted to sleep. Then I forced myself to eat in order to crash. When I came down, I crashed. I almost literally crashed my car driving home late after work one night because I was coming down hard. No matter how hard I tried to keep my eyes open, they wanted to close. My body craved the sleep I had deprived it for so long.

The summer of tenth grade was when everything got even more intense. We started doing crank heavily. The whole world moved faster. People talked faster, made deals faster, interacted faster. Everyone had huge, dilated pupils. Attitudes were different. People were cranky and irritable. Tension was high and trust was low. It seemed everyone was on their own, searching for the cure, but still we called ourselves friends. Relying on people to get your back, and look out for you, dissolved. Instead you watched your own back.

The meth trailer was the hangout for staying up all night, for days in a row. Playing spades was what we did to pass the time. Chopping lines, playing spades. Breathe out and then in deep. Get the whole line in. As the night went on, the lines got longer and longer. After work, going to the trailer and tweaking became my routine.

By now I was lost in a dark world. I had no idea how I would ever escape. Awake two, three, four days at a time. Longest was a week without sleep. Tweaking for that long you start to freak out, get paranoid, and see the most disturbing things.

So hot. Did someone turn up the heat? It's hot in here. Man, it's hot. I need to take my shirt off. I had the sweats. I sat there and played spades in my bra. It was so hot. I looked across the table. McFoley and Shaq both had sweat running down their forehead. Shaq put his hair in a ponytail; the back of his neck was drenched. Man, it's hot in here. The guys had seen my 4-H ribbons on the wall in my bedroom. They teased me, saying that I had earned them doing bad stuff.

Sadness overtook me. 4-H was something Good Bonnie loved. I hardly knew her anymore. I had earned the ribbons because of my talents and the excellent projects I displayed at the fair. My expertise in youth leadership, citizenship, and showing my cat, Andy. Andy, best friend who knew all of my secrets and loved me anyway. My Andy who lay beside me and allowed me to cry all my tears into his fur, as if absorbing my every hurt. The ribbons were earned honestly and wholeheartedly. These guys only saw Bad Bonnie.

When I felt like no one understood, somehow I felt as though my Andy did. I found Andy as a stray on the street. When I brought him home I hid him in my room for almost a month until my mom found out. Mom was really mad and wanted me to get rid of him. Eventually, my mom caved in and Andy became a part of our family. Andy was my best friend.

At the end of the summer, James and I decided to make some extra money on a big deal of some really good stuff. We put our money together, and I went to an old friend, Peter, for help. Peter gave us the money, but he warned me there would be serious consequences if I screwed him over. James and I drove to the Twin Cities. It took a while to find the guy. We were led to this guy, then that guy. We were given numbers to call and then told to delete them after we called. Each step we took, I got more nervous.

"Who's she? Is she cool? She better be cool," one of the guys questioned James because James brought a girl. Finally we got our stuff. The whole drive back I was completely paranoid. Every car in the rearview mirror caused me to panic, thinking it was the cops. Each digit over the speed limit made me think I was getting pulled over for speeding. At home we had to split it out, getting every bag sold. I was a nervous wreck. At any point, something could go wrong. In the end, it worked. Everything went smoothly. We doubled the money. I could never do a deal again. I feared the consequences of getting caught. That was crazy. I didn't care how good the money was. It was too risky. I can't believe I never got busted by the police. I got caught speeding more than enough times, but never got caught on drugs. I must have been really lucky.

James was also friends with a really freaky guy named Dahmer. James introduced me to him at Samson's house. I had never met Samson either. Both of the guys seemed freaky to me, but then again, I was at the point where I trusted no one. As soon as Dahmer met me, he offered me a big rock in a time bomb. A time bomb was folding a rock of crank in a piece of paper and swallowing it. When the paper dissolved, it left the rock in your stomach as a time bomb.

I took it, then later found myself in a frightening situation. I did not want to do anything with Dahmer. I had been warned that he was dirty and quite possibly had AIDS. He stayed awake for months at a time on tweak. I ended up alone with him, and he threatened to kill me if I didn't make up for the time bomb he gave me earlier.

"Do you ever think about dying?" he asked as he stared seriously at me with all of his freakiness.

Will he really kill me or is he just trying to mess with me? "What's your problem?" He asked. Throw up, I wanted to throw up. I wanted to know where James was because I knew he would get me out of this mess. I couldn't find him. I was scared to death that Dahmer was going to seriously hurt me or kill me. I was really scared, so I gave him what he wanted.

Escape. I want to escape. I feel trapped. This is not my life. I hate what is happening to me and the situations I get caught in. I wanted to get higher and higher so the pain would go away. I wished I could run away and never come back. If I didn't have something so amazing as starting college in the fall to look forward to, I would probably kill myself. I want out, but I don't know how.

I continued to wear a mask. People who knew Good Bonnie would have said everything must be great. Good Bonnie was a success. *A pretend success on drugs.* Little did they know behind the mask was Bad Bonnie who carried deep hurts and found relief in getting high, living this horrible life.

In the fall of my junior year, I started to attend community college full-time, for free. I kept working and trying to keep up with my college classes, responsibilities at home, all my organizations and clubs, and dealing with my stomach problems that no one could figure out. My stomach hurt because the chemicals in meth, like bleach and Drano, were eating holes in my stomach. I knew exactly why it hurt.

I was sixteen, and I had earned the opportunity to go to college free. This was my dream. I knew the drugs were making a mess of things. I figured I could quit drugs when I started college. After all, I didn't want to mess up this college opportunity, so I needed to quit the crap. It had been a long summer and I had partied hard, but now I was going to clean up for college.

The college town was about forty minutes away, so soon after I started, I had the wise idea to move out of my mom's house and into an apartment that would be closer to school. My roommates were users, a couple that I didn't know well. I don't know how I talked my mom into letting me live on my own, but somehow I did. My dad thought I was wasting my time going to college; he never liked the idea.

The rent was cheap, but I still needed to work to pay my bills, and I needed to keep my grades up while in college. Living on my own at sixteen was the greatest sense of freedom I had ever known. I was on my own. I bought my own groceries. Things were okay for a few weeks, but I realized how hard it was not to have the security of my mom's shelter. My bills added up. My roommates ate my groceries and I was out of money to buy more. I went to the food shelf to get food, but my roommates ate that, too. I had to keep working a ton of hours and get my homework done to try to pull the grades. I needed all the tweak I could get, but I didn't have the money and I wanted to stay clean for college.

After two months in the apartment, I felt like my life was spinning out of control. I couldn't handle the bills, and I couldn't handle the roommates. I packed everything into my little car and, in one night, moved home.

The inner battle to do drugs or stay clean was fierce inside of me. It was a struggle I could not win. I sat at the kitchen table. It had been a long night at work. I completed the closing shift, and now I needed to complete my homework for the next day of school. I was so tired. I wished I could go to bed. Bed sounded like a good idea. I needed to keep reading. I had a test the next day. I needed to study. I needed to get a good grade on the test. My eyes throbbed. I struggled to follow each line on the page. I lost my place and started over and over again. *Keep reading. Try to remember.* Bed sounded good. I could get up early and read, and then it would be fresh in my mind. *Don't be silly. I can hardly get out of bed in the morning let alone early.* I would never get up to read. *Keep reading. Follow the words. Try to remember. I need a line. A small line, just enough to keep me awake to read this chapter. I need a line. Just go to bed. No, keep reading. Follow the lines. I can do it with a line. I need a line.* I picked up the phone and called a friend.

"Can you come over and bring me a small bump? I'll make it up to you." I didn't know how I would pay for it, but I could figure it out later. How long until you get here? Fifteen minutes? Deal." *Fifteen minutes to being awake. Fifteen minutes. Stay awake. Keep reading.*

I felt so crabby, so irritated. When people talked to me or got too close, my skin felt like it was crawling. *Get away from me. Leave me alone. Leave me the h--- alone.*

My skin itched. The bugs. The bugs keep crawling on my arms. *Get off of me.*

My life was in a spin. Trapped in a big, spinning nightmare.

The trailer. The meth trailer. There were two that we hung at. I never knew who lived there. The residence changed over so fast. *Who cares who lives here, just give me the stuff, and let me hang out for a while.*

I needed a boost for work. Using at work, on the job. Going in the bathroom. Taking a rock and putting it in my cup of pop, or folding it in a small piece of paper, eating it as a time bomb to dissolve in my stomach. Doing a line in the bathroom. Sniffling, sniffling, sniffling. Trying to help customers. My heartbeat pounding out of my chest. Stay awake, earn more shifts, and earn more money. Work, work, work, work hard. Stay awake for days, go to work, working. Eat something, and then crash.

Spin, spin, spin. My life continued to spin. Awake, awake, awake, two, three, four days at a time. Awake for a week without sleep. Freak out. Get paranoid and see disturbing things.

About half way through my junior year of high school/freshman year of college, things really fell apart fast. My boss called me into his office at work and told me my mood swings were out of control, and he had decided to let me go. I crashed my car and had to figure out how to buy another one. At home my mom and I were fighting violently nearly every day. I was angry and furious almost all the time. I wanted her off my back. She found my plate, straw, and blade one time. I lied. The lies came so easy. The lies flowed out of my mouth. She continued to push until I hit her. I hit my mom, punched her in the back after she turned away. *Stay away, Mom, just stay away. It's for your own good. You have no idea what a mess I'm in.* It was a chain of bad events. I was out of control. My life was complete chaos. The crank was taking over.

A few months later, the college sent my transcript to the high school. It wasn't good. The high school counselor called me in his office and said, "If you can't handle it at college, you are coming back to high school." No! I had worked so hard for this. This was my dream, my ticket out of here. If I wanted to do something really great with my life, this was it. And I was losing everything.

I went home and looked at myself in the mirror. I saw my dilated pupils, my face sunken in. I had lesions and sores from digging on my face during paranoia. No makeup in the world could cover up my face. And my stomach hurt so badly. The drugs were killing me, and now they were killing my dream. Crank was destroying my life. *This is a big, freaking nightmare. I want to wake up. Want it gone.* Only a short time and things were going downhill in a drastic way. I was popular with the guys. I asked for a line of coke, they gave it to me, but this was not what I wanted for my life.

I've got to cut back on doing drugs. Yeah, I'm going to cut way back. Maybe just a little pot, but nothing else. I only smoked pot once in a while because I preferred the powders. I didn't drink much anymore, either, because it was a waste. The powder overpowered the central nervous system and the alcohol had no effect. Drinking wasn't worth wasting the money. So if I cut back to only pot, I thought I could handle it.

A couple weeks went by and I did okay. Then I went with Gabriel to see Sebastian and Hawthorne. I hadn't seen Hawthorne for a while, but I heard he had gotten pretty bad. I tried to stay sober, but before long I gave in.

"C'mon, Laabs," he teased. "What? Do you think you are too good for us now?" I sat and watched. Foily after foily my friends smoked, melted each rock into thin air. Line after line until everything was gone. I joined in. We ran out. Not a problem. Hawthorne picked up the phone and paged Morgan, the dealer. Hawthorne sat on the couch and rocked, rocked, rocked, questioning why Morgan didn't promptly return the call. He continued to rock and questioned more. I was high, but I could still see the paranoia. Only five minutes had passed when the call came. Hawthorne walked in the other room to answer.

"Yeah, can we get some more?" he asked into the phone. In his voice I could hear the fear, the panic. What if the answer is no? What will I do? What would he do? What would I do? Would I freak out? Gabriel was an angel. I could see the shimmer of light around him. Was I seeing stuff that wasn't really there?

I went into the bathroom and locked the door. I sat on the toilet and put my head in my hands. *Why am I here? What am I doing?* I was going to cut back. *I don't want to be here, seeing this. I need help. I need to quit this. Oh God, I need to quit.* I sat on the toilet trying to release the toxins inside. What came out was clear. Everything was clear, and I wasn't sure if it was urine or diarrhea. It was clear.

At the sink, I reached for the soap and turned on the water and looked at the wall behind the sink. I wanted so badly to look up, look up, look in the mirror, see my face. I hated to look at myself in the mirror. An ultra-quick glance was all I could manage these days. I was too ashamed to let my eyes lock with my eyes, to study my face. I turned my hands over and over in the water. My eyes grazed the back of the wall and the bottom edge of the medicine cabinet that held the mirror. I studied the pattern of the wallpaper. *Look, just look. Why? LOOK. Why?* The reflecting is horrible and hopeless. I must have stood there for ten minutes trying to force my eyes to look in the mirror. I couldn't. I wouldn't. I turned off the water, dried my hands, and left the bathroom. *I need to quit, but not tonight. Once again I lost the inner battle. I just couldn't do it.*

I walked through the kitchen. A full pizza sat cold on the counter, the remnants of someone hungry but unable to eat. My stomach groaned. Even if I wanted to eat, I couldn't. I sat on the couch next to Hawthorne. "It's coming," he said. "It will be here soon. Yeah, any minute." Hawthorne paced back and forth, to the window, to the door, window, door, couch, door, window, until Morgan arrived with the stuff.

Another foily, another line, another line. Foily, line, foily, line, pipe, line, foily, bong, beer, foily, line. Eight hours non-stop. Run out. Call Morgan. Get more. Foily, line, line, line, foily, pipe. Spin, spin, spin. Awake, awake, awake. Freak out. See the most disturbing things. Check the door, check the window, door, window. Freak out. Paranoid. Major paranoid. This is insane. I'm going insane. This is too much. Go home, force myself to eat something. Crash.

I was high again. I had class the next morning, and I hadn't studied. I failed the test, and I knew the high school counselor would pull me out of college when he found out. Crap.

I went home and locked myself in my room and sat on my bed. I cried for a long time. Held my Andy and cried my tears into his fur. *How could I have gotten this bad? What happened to Good Bonnie? What happened to the confidence I once had in myself?* I didn't know who to talk to, and I was too scared to tell my parents what a mess I was in. *What if they sent me to that group home again?* I would lose college for sure, but I was already losing it. I saw my Bible sitting on the shelf. *God, I need Jesus so bad right now.*

I slept for a long time as I came down. I spent almost a week in my room, holding my Bible and talking to God. I just rocked back on forth on my bed. It actually felt like demons were coming out of me, and I believe they were. *God, I don't want to be a bad kid. I want to be a good kid. I want to go to college and do some really great things with my life. Please God! Help me be a good kid. Jesus, I need your strength. Help me make better choices and start being a good kid. Please help me stop using drugs. Please, Jesus, help me. Please. Please. Please. Jesus, I need your forgiveness. Please, Jesus, forgive me. Forgive me. Please, Jesus, forgive me.*

I had so many goals I wanted to accomplish and I had big dreams, but I knew I was going to lose everything if I didn't make the choice to quit doing drugs. As I prayed, I began to feel stronger and stronger. There is strength in faith.

I have to quit. I choose to quit. God, if you help me, I can quit. I never want to do drugs again. I don't want to hang out with those people. I want out. Please, God, help me. I need your help. I am going to quit. It was the biggest choice in my life. But achieving my goals was way more important than any party, any drug, and any high. I chose to quit. I chose God. *I don't want to be Bad Bonnie anymore. I want to be Good Bonnie, Better than Good Bonnie, Beautiful Bonnie. God, help me be Beautiful.*

After I came out of my room after that long week, I chose not to talk to anyone who had anything to do with drugs or anything that would keep me from focusing on my goals. Quitting was a choice, so I took one choice at a time and made sure I made the right one every time.

It was hard. Really hard. I'm not going to lie. Every cell in my body craved the powders. I just kept telling myself over and over, "You are done; you are going to do this." I left the rest up to God. I could feel his presence, and I knew I had the strength to keep going.

I was also really lonely. Extremely lonely. All the "friends" I had hung out with were never really my friends; they were just people who shared my drug habit. They called my house, but I refused to take their calls. I enforced a screening policy that my mom and brother followed. All my true friends didn't want anything to do with me, because I had hurt them so much. But I was determined. I studied hard and did all the things Good Bonnie would do, and I did them exceptionally well without Bad Bonnie.

I sat home alone and watched movies almost every weekend. I ate tons of ice cream. I put on weight. I didn't care. I was healthy and eating. My stomach started to feel better and the ulcers went away. I missed James, but I didn't want anything to do with drugs and James came with drugs. I was very lonely, but chose to put my energy into positive things. I excelled in 4-H and FLA. I tried cheerleading my senior year. I replaced party time with positive activities and slowly those new activities brought new friendships. I quit working so hard and committed to making money in honest ways. I refused to steal. Each day sober, each choice I made, I moved further and further from Bad Bonnie.

Slowly the pain and hurt dissolved. What I didn't understand before is, Good Bonnie could have goals and be successful, but with the garbage and misery Bad Bonnie carried, it didn't change anything. Good Bonnie was nothing if Bad Bonnie existed. The ultimate change transpired with the belief and hope that my choices alone could rid Bad Bonnie. It was then my pain truly began to decrease. Belief and hope…conquered the pain. *Whatever it takes.* I did whatever it took. I was done doing drugs. So, each choice I made, no matter how hard it was, one choice at a time, I chose not to do drugs.

I am so glad I made the right choice. I sometimes see the "friends" that I once hung out with. Many of them still do drugs. Their lives are not so great. They have huge financial problems. Some are in jail. Most can't keep a job. I have accomplished many things while some of my former friends have been in jail or prison. I am so glad I quit when I did because only a few months after I quit the *friends* I had been hanging with every day started to get busted. That could have been me.

Chapter 8: Resilience: Protective Factors

The last chapter highlighted the struggles of finding my way as a teenager. I chose to resort to substance abuse as a form of self-medication. However, I ultimately showed great resilience and overcame my situation. In this chapter I will review literature surrounding resilience, and apply it to these memories from my teenage years.

According to Felitti et al. (1998), adolescents with a history of high (four or more categories) ACEs are twice as likely to smoke, seven times more likely to consume alcohol at a young age, and seven times more likely to have had sex before age fifteen. Those with an ACE score of 6 or higher were thirty times more likely to attempt suicide. Those that do rely on alcohol use it as a means to coping with stress rather than for social interactions (Felitti, et al., 1998). The coping mechanisms of adopting unhealthy lifestyle choices shed light on why higher ACE scores are associated with tobacco and illegal drug use, obesity, and sexual promiscuity. When an individual has experienced high levels of trauma, it makes sense to seek ways of numbing the pain.

This probability of high ACEs correlated with risk was unfortunately present in my life. Given my personal ACE score of 9, these correlations mirror my path from childhood adversity into self-medication and coping mechanisms of alcohol, drugs, and promiscuity. I was searching for a way out. I wanted so desperately for the pain to be gone. Getting high presented the opportunity for a temporary numbing, or relief. My life was divided into the two characters of Good Bonnie and Bad Bonnie. While a part of me was comfortable using drugs to cope, there was also a desire within me to succeed and overcome. That desire intrigues me, because I feel it is the very essence upon which my resilience is based.

As defined previously, resilience is the stress-resistant personal quality which permits one to thrive in spite of adversity (Ahern, Ark, & Byers, 2008). We must then determine how resilience is identified. Masten presents this criteria: "Identifying resilience in a person's life requires two kinds of evaluation: judgment about exposure to adversity and judgments about how well the person is doing in the midst or aftermath of the adversity" (Masten A. S., 2014, p. 13). Therefore, measuring resilience depends upon the presence of adversity.

Research on resilience has proliferated over the past 40-50 years and has been grouped by Masten (2014) in four waves. The first wave was definitive in describing resilience and establishing parameters for how it can be measured and described, including predictors and outcomes in response to adversity. The second wave shifted into the process of resilience. Researchers aimed to uncover the process of protective or preventative factors which led to resilience, along with the process of positive development in contrast to risk. Around this time (1980), Positive Youth Development was forming. Prior youth work was focused on youth problems and deficits; PYD is geared towards development of positive characteristics of youth, organized by five C's: competence, confidence, connection, character, caring (Pittman, 2000). This led into the third wave of resilience research which examined interventions promoting resilience intertwined with the continuation of testing theories from the first two waves. Finally, recent interest and advances in genetics and neuroscience are promoting the fourth wave of resilience focusing on the interactions of brain development, stress hormones, and human adaptive systems in the context of nurturing and fostering resilience (Masten A. S., 2014, pp. 6-7).

Arising from the arsenal of research on resilience, the most surprising finding is that resilience is actually quite ordinary and common. According to Masten, "Resilience emerges from commonplace adaptive systems for human development, such as a healthy human brain in good working order; close relationships with competent caring adults; committed families; effective schools and communities; opportunities to succeed; and beliefs in the self, nurtured by positive interactions with the world" (p. 8). It is most often the resources and protective factors which yield to the success of a young person.

Looking back on my life, and my ability to break free, how did I do it? How exactly was I able to cut ties with such a captivating and deep addiction? Resilience research provides a lens to understand, through the protective factors which Masten presents in her appropriately-titled book, *Ordinary Magic*. The figure below presents a short list of widely reported protective factors associated with young people who have exhibited resilience. I will take a closer look by diagnosing each listed item in context of the memoir from the previous chapter.

TABLE 6.1. The "Short List" of Widely Reported Factors Associated with Resilience in Young People and Implicated Adaptive Systems

Resilience factors	Adaptive systems
Effective caregiving and parenting quality	Attachment; family
Close relationships with other capable adults	Attachment; social networks
Close friends and romantic partners	Attachment; peer and family systems
Intelligence and problem-solving skills	Learning and thinking systems of the CNS
Self-control; emotion regulation; planfulness	Self-regulation systems of the CNS
Motivation to succeed	Mastery motivation and related reward systems
Self-efficacy	Mastery motivation
Faith, hope, belief life has meaning	Spiritual and cultural belief systems
Effective schools	Education systems
Effective neighborhoods; collective efficacy	Communities

Note. CNS, central nervous system.

Figure 8.1. The McCloskey Model of Executive Function, Source: *Assessment of Executive Function,* 2009 Copyright McCloskey

Attachment and Close Relationships

Parents and caregivers play a supremely important role in the development of a young child. As the child grows older, the importance of adult relationships within the school, neighborhood and community, including teachers, mentors, coaches, and ministers, play a crucial role in development. Friends and later romantic partners are also latent protective relationships (Masten A. S., 2014, p. 150). These protective relationships were a key component to the development of my resilience. While I believe my parents loved me, the quality of parenting they provided was substandard. However, I had numerous positive adult relationships with teachers and community leaders; three of the most prominent were my foster mom (Chapter 5), the volunteer woman I met while at the group home (Chapter 5), and my confirmation mentor (Chapter 7). These three women displayed unconditional love and support all through my adolescent and young adult years. They assured me I was not a bad kid. I often found myself perplexed as to why they cared about me as much as they did.

Attachment theory was first described by John Bowlby (1982), who viewed attachment as a natural protective system keeping young animals from danger. His idea later transcended to the bond between primary caregiver and newborn. A perceived threat could trigger attachment behaviors such as crying or staying close for comfort. Thus attachment figures afford security for exploration and learning, while separation can present anxiety, reunion will bring relief and comfort (Masten A. S., 2014). My parents may not have provided secure attachment relationships to foster resilience but thankfully I did have the other three close nurturing relationships with adults who could provide the emotional security I needed.

In addition to positive adult relationships, I also had a special closeness with my cat. There is something to be said for the comfort pets bring us. My cat saw me through so many sad days. I am so glad I had a pet when my life was so challenging. Philip Tedeschi, professor and executive director of the Institute for Human-Animal Connection within the University of Denver, states that "fostering resiliency, through animal care can increase protective factors for children" (Elvove, Tedeschi, & Brandes, 2015). While there is very little research surrounding the connection to pets and resilience in childhood, I strongly believe that pets provide attachment and can play an important part in promoting resilience in a similar way to how animal therapy is widely accepted as a comfort for many other conditions.

Intelligence and Problem-Solving Skills

Intelligence has proven to be a protective influence in high adversity and is associated with high competence. Resilience does not require a high level of intelligence. However, higher intelligence can provide stronger cognitive skills relating to problem solving and navigating difficult life challenges (Masten A. S., 2014). I have never considered myself highly intelligent, but perhaps slightly above average intelligence. As discussed in Chapter Six, while my executive functions skills relating to interpersonal issues presented issues, I was always capable of doing well academically. Additionally, I have always seemed able to navigate problem solving through difficult life challenges. There were many times I was not sure of the steps I should take to solve a problem, but most importantly I always seemed to have a good idea of who to ask for help to accomplish goals. I think knowing who to seek for help is very crucial in terms of resilience.

Self-Control

Self-regulation, as introduced in Chapter Six, stands out as one of the executive function skills in which I struggled. As I grew older, my self-regulation skills did develop more. Perhaps it was aging and normal maturity of the brain. Perhaps it was the therapy, group home or other interventions I received which played a role in its development. As learned previously, children growing up in severe adversity can have greater deficiencies in executive function skills. However, those executive function skills can be retrained and strengthened over time. It is important to learn how to deal with and learn from failures. Therefore, interventions focused on improving executive function skills should play a vital role in promoting resilience.

Motivation

From the earliest age I can recall ambitions and desires to make an imprint on the world. I wanted to succeed, which is why I think the youth organizations such as 4-H, Future Leaders of America, and others were especially transformative to my personal development. These organizations provided opportunities for mastery and accomplishment. In his book *Self-Efficacy*, Albert Bandura (1997) explains that striving for competence is motivated by the outcomes of competent actions shaped by learning opportunities and a sense of efficacy that develops gradually with experiences. Therefore, self-efficacy derives from the experience of overcoming challenges. A strong sense of self-efficacy affords perseverance in adversity, and likely leads towards success over failure (Masten A. S., 2014). Completing various 4-H projects presented appropriate challenges, accompanied by positive emotions at completion. In the long term they fostered my resilience by increasing my self-efficacy and providing positive adult interactions through these opportunities. Together, these positive experiences allowed me to create and believe in the concept of Good Bonnie.

Faith

Throughout the memoir chapters, glimpses of my spiritual faith come into play. There were definite times when I found myself questioning or angry towards God. However, I always found peace and tranquility in my beliefs. Masten notes that "resilience is associated with hope, optimism, faith, and belief that life has meaning" (p. 164). I agree. In my own times of suffering I seemed to view it through a lens of meaning, or purpose. In the end, I feel that faith was a transformative epiphany that afforded me the strength to ultimately break free from the chains of drugs.

Microsystems and Macrosystems

Individual adaptive systems are influenced through continual interaction and exposure across the environments of family, school, community, and neighborhood. Bronfenbrenner (1979) developed Ecological Systems Theory, which identified five levels of environmental factors which impacted individual growth and development (see Figure 8.2). The relation of these systems to resilience is a newer concept in resilience research.

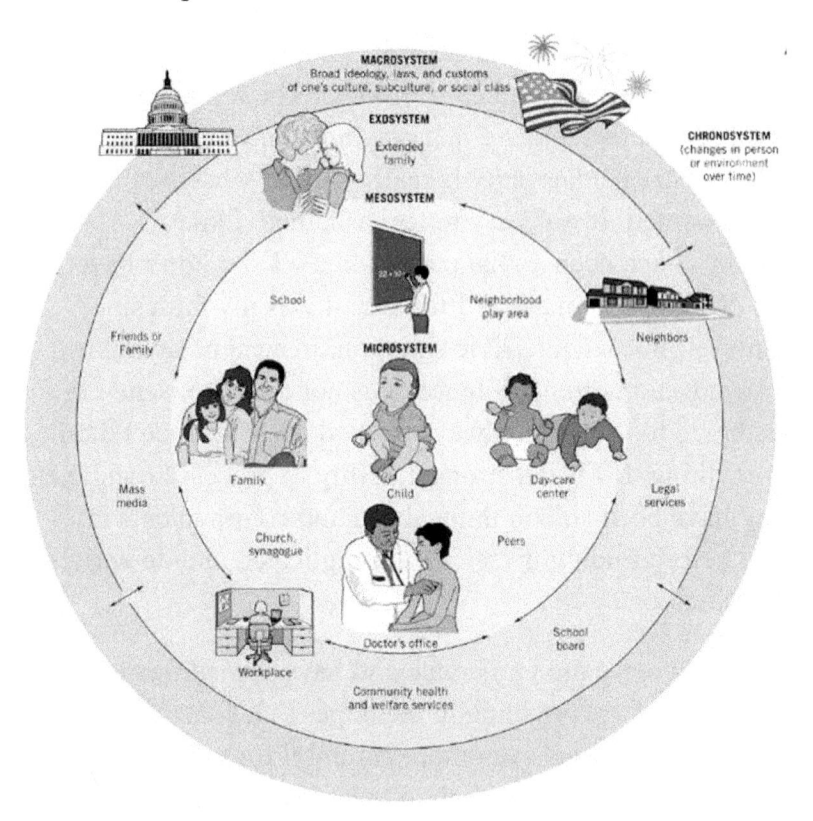

Figure 8.2. Bronfrenbrenner Model of Ecological Systems. (Bronfrenbrenners Ecological Systems Theory, 2014)

Relationships and experiences within and across these systems provide valuable larger resources to foster individual resources. However, I think taking note of the process through which one learns to navigate the unwritten rules of boundaries within these systems may offer new ideas towards fostering individual resilience.

    For example, now that I am an adult and have a more concrete view of the situation, it is obvious to me that I was raped. This is what is called *gray rape*. The term refers to sexual encounters that are in a gray area between consent and denial, where neither party is really sure of what the other person wanted. It was easy to feel ashamed. I knew I shouldn't have been at that party. I knew I shouldn't have been drinking, so in a way I felt like it was my fault since I put myself in such a terrible situation. Instead of saying no, I froze and said nothing. Silence does not equal consent, nor does being too drunk. I always blamed myself, since I didn't say anything. If I had a stronger ability to process boundaries, I may have been able to think ahead and communicate my needs before finding myself in a complicated and downright scary situation.

    When we are vulnerable and have low self-esteem, we will do almost anything in the hopes that someone will like us. I think this is even more common for girls that seek attention from guys. I so desired to be loved and cared for by a guy. Therefore, I was willing to do almost anything for male attention. I also thought if I could party like they did, they would like me. All I ever did was hurt myself. I had no sense of personal boundaries. Now when I look back, I can clearly see how I allowed these guys to take advantage of me. When young people have a strong sense of how to define and communicate healthy personal boundaries it will promote long-term resilience.

My Resilience

How do we know when an individual is resilient? While behavioral studies tend to focus on symptoms and outcomes related to mental health, developmental studies focus on an individual adaptation in relation to age appropriate tasks or expectations as stereotypically determined by society. Erik Erikson (1963, 1968) explored these age appropriate tasks in the context of identity formation. These salient development tasks (see Figure 8.3) are essential milestones geared toward judging how an individual is doing at a particular age. Young children are quite oblivious to the judgments surrounding this society driven criteria, however, adolescents are typically aware and tend to even evaluate themselves according to their personal competence regarding these tasks (Masten A. S., 2014).

My goal in resilience research is to uncover the possibilities of efforts proven to strengthen and foster adaptation. While many of Masten's resilience factors above resonate with my story, they cannot provide an absolute formula as individual cases are vastly unique.

My final realization that I needed to change my life is consistent with Masten's description of a late bloomer. Attending post-secondary while technically a high school student presented just the window of opportunity I needed. Soon after the freedom to move away presented another window of opportunity and solidified the emergence of resilience as I blossomed as a late bloomer. According to Masten, "The phenomenon of "late-bloomers" in resilience may reflect the late surge of capacity for self-reflections and planning, combined with the opportunities that societies may offer for finding a new path in the transition to adulthood" (Masten A. S., 2014, p. 159). Not only do late bloomers exhibit a surge or strong desire to change, they also delight with pride transcending from the active choice of making the change (Masten A. S., 2014). This notion resonates closely with my story. Clearly, I had a strong motivation to change and indeed I am very proud of the choice I made.

Infancy period
Forming attachment bonds with primary caregivers
Learning to sit and crawl
Emerging: learning to communicate by gesture and language

Toddler and preschool period
Waning: crawling
Learning to walk and run
Learning to speak the language of the family
Obeying simple commands
Learning to play with other children
Emerging: self-control of attention and impulses

Early school years
Attending school and behaving appropriately
Learning to read and write the language of the community
Getting along with other children
Respecting and obeying elders
Emerging: making close friends

Adolescence
Adjusting to physical maturation
Successful transitioning to secondary schooling
Following the rules and laws of society
Committing to a religion
Forming close friendships
Emerging: exploring identity, romantic relationships, work

Early adulthood
Waning: academic achievement
Achieving a cohesive sense of self
Forming a close romantic relationship
Contributing to family livelihood through work in the home or community
Establishing a career
Establishing a family
Emerging: civic engagement

Figure 8.3. Salient Development Tasks

My memoir presents a single-case account of resilience. Single-case, person-focused models of resilience, according to Masten, although difficult for generalizability, provide a rich variety and complexity of human life. Single case studies typically highlight "late bloomers", who turn their life around in the transition to adulthood, during a period of development which offers a window of opportunity provided by advanced schooling or training, military service, job opportunities, positive romantic relationships, involvement in a religious organization, or the legal freedom to move and take ownership of life (Masten A. S., 2014). Sharing one's story appears to be a therapeutic form of gaining control of past traumatic experiences. Resilience persists, but fluctuates and does not guarantee a smooth course through life (Masten A. S., 2014).

In my situation, I had several precedent protective factors, such as positive adult relationships, strong self-efficacy and motivation, good problem-solving capabilities, and faith that operated at different strengths (see Figure 8.4) but all promoted strong resilience. While I did not have every protective factor on Masten's short list, those that I did have were quite prominent. While this equation worked for me, other resilient individuals may have a different equation of prominent factors.

- Positive Adult Relationships
- Motivation/Self-efficacy
- Faith
- Intelligence/Problem Solving Skills
- Self-Control
- Effective Schools

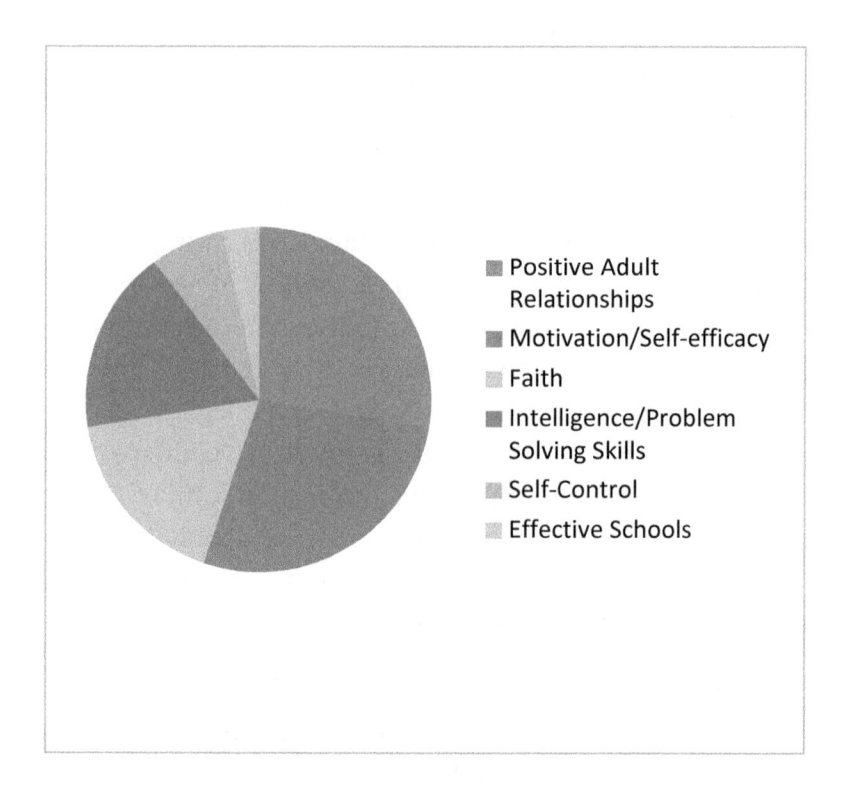

Figure 8.4. Prominent Protective Factors in My Life

Resilience is not a trait, but rather multiple characteristics associated with stronger adaptation (Masten A. S., 2014). Whether an individual succeeds or fails, first depends on the criteria for determining success, as discussed above. In order for resilience to be visible, adversity must also occur. One cannot exhibit resilience if there are not challenges to overcome. How resilient an individual may be depend on the protective factors.

Chapter 9: Behavior Intervention

Now, several years after the events described in the memoir chapters, I have become a teacher. In this position, I have the ability to utilize my understanding of Adverse Childhood Experiences and the effects of brain development and executive function. One such use is creating effective and compassionate behavior interventions, which I describe in this chapter. These interventions both affect my students and continue to shape me.

Based on my retrospective understanding and theoretical education, I created and administered a hybrid behavior intervention program for Tier 2 students as categorized by the Positive Behavior Interventions Supports (PBIS) (Lindsey, 2008). Participants for the intervention program were determined through criterion sampling. They also needed to be in fourth or fifth grades and not receiving special services (IEP). Specific students were then identified by means of the prior year School Wide Information System (SWIS) data indicating referrals and suspensions, classroom observation, and recommendation of classroom teachers. After students were identified as candidates for behavior intervention, parent permission slips were sent home.

Participants were screened for their Adverse Childhood Experiences (ACEs) score (see Figure 2.2) to determine the level of trauma a student has faced as well as weigh in on risk factors and protective factors in their lives. I am greatly intrigued by the recent research which relies on ACE score as a predictor of how a young person may thrive or struggle, specifically in learning settings. The ACE Study is taking a place on the forefront as more organizations are paying closer attention to the effects of childhood trauma. The National Child Traumatic Stress Network (NCTSN) survey reported that interpersonal victimization in the family home was the most prevalent form of childhood trauma being treated by mental health professionals (Spinazzola, et al., 2005). In June of 2005, the Massachusetts Department of Education reported data collected from informal surveys of 450 students who were enrolled in alternative education programs. The report declared that 90 percent of the students reported histories of trauma exposure, with the majority reporting exposure to more than one type of trauma. Of the sample, 41% reported family violence; 46% reported physical, emotional, or sexual abuse; 39% reported neglect; and 16% were living in foster care or out of the home placements (Burns, 2005). In review of studies on the overlap between domestic violence and child maltreatment, Eldeson (1999) found that where one form of family violence (neglect, violence, abuse) occurs, another form will also occur in 30-60% of cases. It has also been concluded that familial alcoholism occurs mostly commonly with family violence (Ritter, Stewart, Bernet, & Coe, 2002). In later chapters, I will go into further detail and apply ACE scoring to my own life.

Following ACE and Resilience scoring, I had classroom teachers complete the Assessment of Lagging Skills and Unsolved Problems (ALSUP) survey (see Figure 2.3) to identify lagging skills and unsolved problems. Then students worked with me to choose three main goals by identifying the three most immediate areas of concern on the

ALSUP. This information became the Plan Flowchart, a design to help keep track of the unsolved problems currently being worked on. The flowchart was then shared with the parent and classroom teachers to ensure a collaborative approach.

Overview of the Goal Setting process and Specific Measurable Achievement while Relevant and Timebound (SMART) goals were covered with the students. Students set additional life goals for 1 year, 5 years, and 10 years in order to frame the three behavioral goals as steps toward long-term goals. In addition, we began working on daily and weekly goals as steps towards our three behavioral goals. Each student journaled daily and weekly goals relative to their three main goals and complete bi-weekly check-ins and reflections. Classroom teachers signed daily indicating whether the goal was met. Rewards were available for students who met weekly goals. Journals also included daily notes between the student and teachers in response and reflection to daily occurrences.

154

ADVERSE CHILDHOOD EXPERIENCES (ACEs)
10 QUESTION SCREENING TOOL

The ACEs 10 Question Screening Tool is an abbreviated version of the ACEs Family Health History Questionnaires and Health Appraisal Questionnaires available at http://www.cdc.gov/ace/questionnaires.htm
A comprehensive list of validated youth trauma screening and assessment tools are maintained on the NCTSN Measures Review available at: http://www.nctsn.org/resources/online-research/measures-review

FINDING YOUR ACEs SCORE
WHILE YOU WERE GROWING UP, DURING YOUR FIRST 18 YEARS OF

#	Question	Circle	One	If YES Enter 1
1	Did a parent or other adult in the household often or very often swear at you, insult you, put you down, or humiliate you? OR act in a way that made you afraid that you might be physically hurt?	Yes	No	
2	Did a parent or other adult in the household often or very often push, grab, slap, or throw something at you? OR ever hit you so hard that you had marks or were injured?	Yes	No	
3	Did an adult or person at least 5 years older than you ever touch or fondle you or have you touch their body in a sexual way? OR attempt or actually have oral, anal, or vaginal intercourse with you?	Yes	No	
4	Did you often or very often feel that: No one in your family loved you or thought you were important or special? OR your family didn't look out for each other, feel close to each other, or support each other?	Yes	No	
5	Did you often or very often feel that you didn't have enough to eat, had to wear dirty clothes, and had no one to protect you? OR your parents were too drunk or high to take care of you or take you to the doctor if you needed it?	Yes	No	
6	Were your parents ever separated or divorced?	Yes	No	
7	Was your mother or stepmother often or very often pushed, grabbed, slapped, or had something thrown at her? OR sometimes, often, or very often kicked, bitten, hit with a fist, or hit with something hard? OR ever repeatedly hit at least a few minutes or threatened with a gun or knife?	Yes	No	
8	Did you live with anyone who was a problem drinker or alcoholic or who used street drugs?	Yes	No	
9	Was a household member depressed or mentally ill, or did a household member attempt suicide?	Yes	No	
10	Did a household member go to prison?	Yes	No	

NOW ADD UP YOUR "YES" ANSWERS. THIS IS YOUR ACEs SCORE.

Figure 2.1. Adverse Childhood Experiences 10 Question Screening Tool, *Adolescent Provider Toolkit*, retrieved from http://acestoohigh.com/got-your-ace-score/. Copyright 2013 By Adolescent Health Working Group

ASSESSMENT OF LAGGING SKILLS & UNSOLVED PROBLEMS (Rev. 12/5/08)

Child's Name _____ Date _____ Person Completing Form _____

LAGGING SKILLS

	Never	Sometimes	Often	Always
1. Difficulty handling transitions, shifting from one mindset or task to another	0	1	2	3
2. Difficulty doing things in a logical sequence or prescribed order	0	1	2	3
3. Difficulty persisting on challenging or tedious tasks	0	1	2	3
4. Poor sense of time	0	1	2	3
5. Difficulty reflecting on multiple thoughts or ideas simultaneously	0	1	2	3
6. Difficulty maintaining focus	0	1	2	3
7. Difficulty considering the likely outcomes or consequences of actions (impulsive)	0	1	2	3
8. Difficulty considering a range of solutions to a problem	0	1	2	3
9. Difficulty expressing concerns, needs, or thoughts in words	0	1	2	3
10. Difficulty understanding what is being said	0	1	2	3
11. Difficulty managing emotional response to frustration so as to think rationally	0	1	2	3
12. Chronic irritability and/or anxiety significantly impede capacity for problem solving or heighten frustration	0	1	2	3
13. Difficulty seeing the "grays"/concrete, literal, black-and-white, thinking	0	1	2	3
14. Difficulty deviating from rules, routine	0	1	2	3
15. Difficulty handling unpredictability, ambiguity, uncertainty, novelty	0	1	2	3
16. Difficulty shifting from original idea, plan, or solution	0	1	2	3
17. Difficulty taking into account situational factors that would suggest the need to adjust a plan of action	0	1	2	3
18. Inflexible, inaccurate interpretations/cognitive distortions or biases (e.g., "Everyone's out to get me," "Nobody likes me," "You always blame me," "It's not fair," "I'm stupid")	0	1	2	3
19. Difficulty attending to or accurately interpreting social cues/poor perception of social nuances	0	1	2	3
20. Difficulty starting conversations, entering groups, connecting with people/lacking other basic social skills	0	1	2	3
21. Difficulty seeking attention in appropriate ways	0	1	2	3
22. Difficulty appreciating how his/her behavior is affecting other people	0	1	2	3
23. Difficulty empathizing with others, appreciating another person's perspective or point of view	0	1	2	3
24. Difficulty appreciating how s/he is coming across or being perceived by others	0	1	2	3

UNSOLVED PROBLEMS

HOME	Never	Sometimes	Often	Always
1. Waking up/getting out of bed in the morning	0	1	2	3
2. Completing morning routine/getting ready for school	0	1	2	3
3. Sensory hypersensitivities	0	1	2	3
4. Starting or completing homework or a particular academic task	0	1	2	3
5. Food quantities/choices/preferences/timing	0	1	2	3
6. Time spent in front of a screen (TV, video games, computer)	0	1	2	3
7. Going to/getting ready for bed at night	0	1	2	3
8. Boredom	0	1	2	3
9. Sibling interactions	0	1	2	3
10. Cleaning room/completing household chores	0	1	2	3
11. Taking medicine	0	1	2	3
12. Riding in car/wearing seatbelt	0	1	2	3

SCHOOL	Never	Sometimes	Often	Always
1. Shifting from one specific task to another (specify)	0	1	2	3
2. Getting started on/completing class assignments (specify)	0	1	2	3
3. Interactions with a particular classmate/teacher (specify)	0	1	2	3
4. Behavior in hallway/at recess/in cafeteria/on school bus/waiting in line (specify)	0	1	2	3
5. Talking at appropriate times	0	1	2	3
6. Academic tasks/demands, e.g., writing assignments (specify)	0	1	2	3
7. Handling disappointment/losing at a game/not coming in first/not being first in line (specify)	0	1	2	3

OTHERS (list)	Never	Sometimes	Often	Always
1.	0	1	2	3
2.	0	1	2	3
3.	0	1	2	3
4.	0	1	2	3

©Center for Collaborative Problem Solving, 2008

Figure 2.3. Assessment of Lagging Skills and Unsolved Problems, *Center for Collaborative Problem Solving,* Copyright 2008

Bi-weekly small group sessions focused on student's goal process, choices, suggestions for success, and skills for improvement and "Coping Power" strategies. The Coping Power Program is a preventive intervention delivered to at-risk children in the late elementary school and early middle school years. Coping Power is based on an empirical model of risk factors for substance use and delinquency and addresses key factors including: social competence, self-regulation, and positive parental involvement (Lochman, Wells, & Lenhart, 2006).

Comparing students' quantitative and qualitative intervention data through an autoethnographic lens encompassing my personal reflections of my childhood and professional experience should ultimately uncover strategies for increasing resilience in survival-based students. The study overall sheds light on the relationship between behavior interventions targeting improvement of executive function skills and increased level of resilience. In advance of data collection, I anticipated highs and lows in the students' classroom behaviors throughout the intervention with explosive behaviors tapering off towards the end. Evidence of such highs and lows were to be recorded in students' daily goal/point sheets, and journal comments from classroom teachers. I also expected to see more developed and deeper reflective individual journaling from students. Executive function skills were to also indicate growth from the beginning to the end of the intervention on the Assessment of Lagging Skills and Unsolved Problems (ALSUP) Lickert scale. Finally, the results from this intervention were expected to confirm both the results from my personal experience and the literature on resilience.

This curriculum was implemented at an elementary school in the metropolitan area of Minnesota. The hybrid intervention program I designed included Collaborative Problem Solving, Coping Skills development, goal setting and boundaries awareness, intertwined with meta-cognitive processing, in addition to the existing PBIS structure. I choose these because they were in my opinion the best resources for assessing and strengthening executive function skills.

This particular inner-city Elementary school is known for high referral, detention and suspension rates. My belief is the high level of explosive and survival-based behaviors at this school is directly related to level of trauma and ACEs that these students have faced. I relied on my experience from previous efforts to reach students in survival mode and to combat the effects of ACEs in formal education settings.

If we tentatively accept the research and experiences discussed in previous chapters, then students who have experienced high levels of ACEs have probably developed cognitive differences as a result of being in survival mode. In addition, they have not developed the ability process meta-cognitively. Studies by Masten (2012) and Shonkoff (2012) show that trauma and ACEs are correlated with a lack of brain development, specifically of the prefrontal cortex. If resilience and self-efficacy are indeed related to executive function, then it would make sense for behavior interventions to be designed to aim at improving executive function skills.

There is more at stake for the students at my school than classroom discipline and grades. The intervention then, should result an increase of a survival-based student's level of overall health as well as resilience and self-efficacy, and reduce the explosive behaviors the student exhibits in the classroom. Students in survival mode are likely to exhibit explosive behavior in the classroom and require specific behavior interventions (i.e. caring adults who will help them determine the lagging skills they must develop) in attempt to correct the behavior. I sought to incorporate this model into my classroom intervention.

Collaborative Problem Solving

There are three main components to the Collaborative Problem-Solving program, as designed by Greene (2008). First, the Assessment of Lagging Skills and Unsolved Problems (ALSUP) identified lagging skills and unsolved problems. Second, the Plan B Flowchart helped keep track of the unsolved problems currently being worked on and where each student was in the process of solving them. Third, the Plan B Cheat Sheet provided key components to keep in mind while doing Plan B.

Process Steps, Overview and Timeline

September

1. Students were identified by means of the prior year SWIS (School Wide Information System) data, observation, and consultation with other classroom teachers. Students did not qualify if they were already receiving Special Education support.

2. After students were identified as candidates for CPS, a parent permission slip and ALSUP were sent home. Parents were also called to have a conversation about the goals of CPS and begin the home connection piece. Nineteen fourth and fifth grade student participated in the program.

3. Classroom teachers also completed and ALSUP to provide their perspective.

October

4. Students began the CPS group time with an interview and getting to know you time. They were then given a composition notebook to use as a personal journal.

5. Once all ALSUP forms had been collected, students identified 3 main behavioral goals to focus on, collaboratively with me. These 3 goals were then documented in the Plan B Flowchart. The flowchart was then shared with the parent and classroom teachers to ensure a collaborative approach. The students wrote their 3 big goals in their journal.

6. Overview of the Goal Setting process and SMART goals was covered with the students. Students set additional life goals for 1 year, 5 years, and 10 years out and begin to understand that the 3 behavioral goals are steps towards the long-term goals and in addition- we began working on daily and weekly goals as steps towards our 3 main behavioral goals.

7. Each student began journaling daily and weekly goals relative to their 3 main goals and completed bi-weekly

check-ins and reflections. The point sheet was used to track weekly short-term goals and progress.

November

8. Bi-weekly small group sessions focused on student's goal process, choices, suggestions for success, and skills for improvement and incorporated "Coping Power" strategies. The Coping Power strategies helped students to develop and improve skills such as, anger management, problem solving, impulse control, friendship skills, etc. The Coping Power Program is a preventive intervention delivered to at-risk children in the late elementary school and early middle school years. Coping Power is based on an empirical model of risk factors for substance use and delinquency and addresses key factors including: social competence, self-regulation, and positive parental involvement (Coping Power, 2006).

9. As I learned more about Adverse Childhood Experiences (ACE Scores), I also interviewed each student to determine their ACE score.

April

10. The AULSUP was again completed in the spring, and the Plan B flowchart was adjusted accordingly for both assessment and evaluation of progress. I compiled individual AULSUP scores into a spreadsheet and color coded them for to make an easy visual of progress. I refer to this color-coded spreadsheet as a "heat map".

    My overall goal with this intervention was to build and administrate a behavior intervention program for troubled students, but I learned even more about behaviors as I worked on it. I researched and implemented tools for strengthening executive function with students. I also gained an understanding of which elements used in this behavior intervention program were the most effective. In was reminded that in relating to explosive students, I may not be able to anticipate until I really get started and learn along the way what works and doesn't work.

The Experience in Detail

To begin, I met with the school social worker, and school psychologist in September to discuss possibilities for program structure and confirm where our efforts would collaborate and not overlap. We also discussed potential students and agreed on the criterion that students must not already have an intervention in place (IEP), and lastly narrowed my focus to fourth and fifth grade students.

Next, I reviewed the previous year's SWIS data, conducting a search for students with more than 50 behavioral referrals in the previous school year. I followed this up with classroom observations and requested fourth and fifth grade teachers to identify student candidates for the program.

Finally, in October, I began meeting with students. I began with a student interview sheet to help get to know students and begin building relationships. Students were told I would be meeting with them because they were identified as students who could use some extra help outside the classroom because they struggled to manage behavior. Students were sent home a parent permission form and ALSUP. Phone calls home to explain the program were also made. I was very surprised at how difficult it was to get the signed form back; some students took up to 6 weeks to return it. I think the general assumption was parents felt as though this was a form of special education assessment because of the ALSUP. Phone calls explaining otherwise to parents seemed to help. Only one student was a solid "No" in the program. I had fifteen students in the program: eight 4th graders and seven 5th graders, eight boys, and seven girls.

I provided the students with composition notebooks, which served as journals. Each student filled out long-term/short-term goal sheets. Each student had three ALSUP's, which were conducted to gain an understanding of student behavior. I completed observations of students during classroom learning, another from a parent's, third, classroom teachers also completed ALSUPs. Individually, I compiled and reviewed the three ALSUP questionnaires with each student, and simultaneously filled in the Plan B Flowchart as the students helped to isolate three major problems areas which translated to main goals they wanted to focus on. After confirming these goals areas with the classroom teachers, more specific information in regard to solving these problems was gathered. Students also gave input and ultimately a collaborative problem was developed.

By November of the school year, my relationships with the students seemed to be developing well and becoming very beneficial to their success, they were eager to select goals each week. Students selected three goals for the week and earned a Yes or a No if they met the goal for the day. Goals included being respectful, prepared, listening, and not being disruptive. About half of the students were able to earn success with this system. In November the system was changed to a scale of 1 to 5 points possible for the day's goals. This helped for students who had a bad moment during the day to be able to get back on track for the rest of the day—therefore making the reward more attainable.

Typical bi-weekly meetings consisted of the students coming in a small group of 2 or 3 to my room. We would start by looking at the goals in the journal and the students would share with me how their day was going. Next, we would have a brief lesson from the Coping Power program. These lessons were usually about anger management, relationship skills, organizational skills, or impulse control. While the students would complain about having to do any writing, they seemed to enjoy these lessons. To finish our session, we would revisit their weekly goals and discuss what they would need to do to achieve them. Last, I often wrote a brief motivational message in their journal and sent them back to class.

This schedule worked well unless the students came late, and the next group came early, or the days when students needed a bit longer to talk. Having more than three students at a time would get distracting. The students would be less authentic and limit their answers when there were too many people in the group.

Friday was reward and reset day. Students would come in, glue in a new goal sheet for the upcoming week and select their goals. If they earned a reward, they would receive it then. In the beginning I would tell students what the Friday reward (special treat, reward time, movie, etc.) would be at the start of the week in hopes that they would have something to look forward to and get excited for. However, in January, I began keeping the Friday reward as a surprise.

Another innovation occurred when I tried having the girls come to reward time together. I was hoping to build community among the girls, and it allowed time to discuss items that they were more comfortable discussing without boys. We did our nails and this seemed to go well. This worked well enough that we started a boy's group too. For boy's time we usually built something like catapults; this was great fun. However, three or four of the students did not participate because the teachers would not let them come at the designated time.

I documented this experience in several ways: by journaling weekly and taking notes on the process and development of this program, and by writing out my response to what I learned and how the readings and researched helped to shape my experience. While I had hoped to have students create short videos highlighting digital stories, and envisioned showing clips of the students Digital Voice documentaries and including pieces of learning organized together to tell the story of this project, the reality is, this piece did not have the time allowed to produce such documentation, as I did not have the time or resources to work edit the videos with the students.

Effectiveness was also measured by student achievement of goals, responsiveness and application to skill training and development, and Likert scores on the ALSUPs.

In addition, progress was monitored and informed through monthly conversation with classroom teachers, behavior staff observations, and student feedback. Lastly, a review of the SWIS data will also indicated a decline in school referrals and suspensions.

The following are several vignettes of my experiences with anonymized students. I choose to highlight stories that exhibited the most progress throughout the program and those that were the most powerful to my learning.

Sandie

I quickly noticed that Sandie could become very difficult, moody and shut down when she was held accountable, and especially when she did not get her way. We were working hard on rebounding from a mistake and not letting it ruin her whole day or week. She seemed to be very embarrassed when she made a mistake and was unable to continue. One day she ripped my bulletin board, another day she ripped a page out of her journal. In time she was able to turn her mood around, but it often took a long while.

"Sandie, what do you think you struggle with the most?" I asked.

"Well, I think I could be nicer sometimes, but it's hard when I don't get what I want."

"Your teacher shared that you sometimes yell at other students, bully them, or tease them, does that seem true?

"Ya, like I said, they make me mad."

"What things make you mad?"

"I asked Jessica if I could use her pencil. She said no. It made me really mad. I asked nice and she said no. So, I took the pencil anyway."

"Do you think Jessica should have let you use the pencil?"

"Yes, because I asked nicely."

"Does Jessica have a right to say no?"

"I guess, but she shouldn't say no because I asked nicely."

"It was respectful of you to ask to use the pencil rather than just taking it. However, she has a right to say no. Just like you have the right to say no when someone requests to use an item that belongs to you. I can see how her saying no made you feel angry. I wonder if you are really angry or embarrassed?"

"What do you mean?"

"I think initially you were angry, and that's why you took the pencil. After you took it though, I think you realized it was not the right thing to do, so you are embarrassed. You might feel embarrassed because you know what you did was wrong but you don't know how to fix it?"

"Yes, you're right. I just got so mad."

"Perhaps you can ask yourself if you are angry or embarrassed."

I started to jot down a simple flowchart in her journal.

"If you are angry, then ask yourself how you can calm down in a safe way. If you are embarrassed, ask yourself how you can solve it before it gets worse. If you don't know, ask a teacher or adult, say "I'm stuck, please help me fix this." Does that make sense?"

This seemed to resonate with Sandie. There were several times following where she became moody again, particularly after she had made a mistake. It seemed to help if I asked her if she was angry or embarrassed. Most often she would continue to be in a foul mood. I would continue to talk out loud about anger versus embarrassment, how this was a normal reaction to having made a mistake, how to stop rather than making it worse, and how our actions were affecting others. It helped, and Sandie was able to transition out of her bad moods in much less time.

Sandie was one of the hardest, yet most rewarding students to work with. She is an only child and her home life clearly fueled her behaviors. Sandie could be all sugar and spice, until she doesn't get her way. Then she could be mean. We spent the entire school year working on this. Sadly, most of the behaviors Sandie exhibits appear to be a direct reflection of her mother's actions and attitudes. Her mother treated the teachers and staff in a similar manner; she was very sweet until she did not get the answer she wanted and then resorted to yelling, swearing, and intimidation. Her mother had been in jail numerous times, and when she was out she danced at the club for income. Her father was in prison. Sandie's ACE score was 7 out of 10.

Throughout the intervention Sandie and I worked on improving interactions with others (classmates and teachers), specifically considering outcomes, impulsiveness, and understanding how her behavior affected others. In addition, we discussed academic motivation, getting started on work, and persisting on challenging tasks. Sandie hated completing her math work, and as a result was falling behind the rest of her class.

Sandie showed wonderful improvements throughout the intervention. Her ALSUP improved 18 points going from 71 in the fall to 53 in the spring. Her school referrals had declined from 15 write-ups the previous school year, to only 6 in the current year.

Lagging Skills	Fall	Spring
1. Difficulty handling transitions, shifting from one mindset or task to another.	2	1
2. Difficulty doing things in a logical sequence or prescribed order.	2	1
3. Difficulty persisting on challenging or tedious tasks.	1	3
4. Poor sense of time.	2	0
5. Difficulty reflecting on multiple thoughts or ideas simultaneously.	1	1
6. Difficulty maintaining focus.	3	2
7. Difficulty considering the likely outcomes or consequences of actions (impulsive).	3	2
8. Difficulty considering a range of solutions to a problem.	3	3
9. Difficulty expressing concerns, needs, or thoughts in words.	1	2
10. Difficulty understanding what is being said.	1	1
11. Difficulty managing emotional response to frustration so as to think rationally.	3	2
12. Chronic irritability and/or anxiety significantly impede capacity for problem-solvi	3	2
13. Difficulty seeing the "grays"/concrete, literal, black-and-white, thinking.	3	2
14. Difficulty deviating from rules, routine.	1	1
15. Difficulty handling unpredictability, ambiguity, uncertainty, novelty.	1	0
16. Difficulty shifting from original idea, plan, or solution.	1	0
17. Difficulty taking into account situational factors that would suggest the need to ad	2	0
18. Inflexible, inaccurate interpretations/cognitive distortions or biases (e.g., "Everyo "Nobody likes me," "You always blame me, "It's not fair," "I'm stupid")	3	3
19. Difficulty attending to or accurately interpreting social cues/poor perception of so	3	2
20. Difficulty starting conversations, entering groups, connecting with people/lacking	3	1
21. Difficulty seeking attention in appropriate ways.	3	3
22. Difficulty appreciating how his/her behavior is affecting other people.	3	3
23. Difficulty empathizing with others, appreciating another person's perspective or p	3	2
24. Difficulty appreciating how s/he is coming across or being perceived by others.	1	2

SCHOOL- Unsolved Problems

1. Shifting from one specific task to another.	3	1
2. Getting started on/completing class assignments.	2	2
3. Interactions with a particular classmate/teacher.	3	3
4. Behavior in hallway/at recess/in cafeteria/on school bus/waiting in line.	2	2
5. Talking at appropriate times.	3	2
6. Academic tasks/demands, e.g., writing assignments.	3	2
7. Handling disappointment/losing at a game/not coming in first/not being first in line	3	1

OTHER- Unsolved Problems

Figure 9.1 Sandie's ALSUP

Deena

Deena responded extremely well to her time with me but she continued to get in trouble in her classroom. She had stolen from teachers on three occasions and been suspended.

"Do you know why you are in trouble?"

"Ya, I got caught stealing."

"What did you steal?"

"Candy, from a teacher. Well I wouldn't have got caught, but somebody snitched on me."

"So, you think taking the candy was ok, if you wouldn't have gotten caught?"

"Well...no, I'm just mad that I got snitched on. Otherwise I won't be in no trouble."

"The point is that you took something that didn't belong to you. Getting caught or not, you still stole something."

"Ya I know. I just can't help it."

Deena had already been caught stealing on three occasions in the first two months of the school year. It was always junk food. It was obvious she had a serious sweet tooth and she had extreme difficulty avoiding the temptation of swiping treats.

"Deena, I used to steal things too."

"How did you stop?"

"Well, I had to think about who my actions were hurting."

"What? Who does a little candy hurt?"

"You are stealing from teachers. I'm a teacher too. We spend quite a bit of money from our own pocket on treats and prizes for students. The school doesn't purchase those things, the teachers do. In a way you are stealing from yourself, too."

"From myself?"

"Yes. When you take something that a teacher has bought with the intention of giving to you as a reward. You are really taking something from yourself, because the teacher will have less to reward you with."

"Oh."

"Do you like it when people take your things?"

"No. I get real mad."

"Try to think about that when you are thinking of taking something."

It baffled me that Deena would steal from other teachers, but she never stole from me. Was it that she held a different respect for me? Did she fear the conversation we would have if I held her accountable?

Along with stealing, Deena had an extreme difficulty with lying. She could look anyone right in the eye and lie. She would be so convinced by her own lies, it was like she didn't even know what the truth was. What she didn't realize is that teachers talked to each other, and they would verify her stories.

"Deena why are you not in uniform?"

"Mr. Doug told me I could change."

"Really? School will not be out for two more hours. Our uniform policy is strict. I find it hard to believe that he would allow you to change."

"He did, Ms. Laabs. He said I could change."

"Are you telling the truth?"

"Ya, I swear."

"If I ask Mr. Doug what will he say?"

"Call him. He will tell you."

I caught Mr. Doug after school.

"Did you tell Deena she could change out of her uniform? She insisted that you did."

"Of course not. She never even asked me," he replied.

Her compulsive lying was irritating. I never quite knew when she was being honest. Almost always I had to reference her stories.

The next week she got in trouble for using Twitter on the school computer. Her consequence was loss of computer privileges for one month. She, of course, lied about this too.

A month later she was doing well. She hadn't stolen anything and was getting better at being honest, or at least changing her story when confronted. Then I saw her after school eating some candy. It was the same type of candy that Mr. Bennet gave out to his students. I questioned her but she insisted she got it from another student. The next day I went to confirm with Mr. Bennet. Of course, he was missing candy from his reward stash and he found a broken pencil shoved in his door, jamming the lock. I was furious. We had been working on not stealing, she was doing well. She was getting so much better at coming forward with the truth too. I was so angry that she insisted the candy come from a student. Mr. Bennet, Mr. Doug, and I had a meeting with Deena. We asked her again to tell us the truth about the candy. Again, and again she insisted the candy came from a friend.

"Do you realize how serious this is? Mr. Doug asked.

"Not only did someone steal from me, but they broke my door lock too. That's breaking and entering." Mr. Bennet added.

"Pre-meditated: that's a term for criminals that plan ahead." Mr. Doug noted.

"That's right, Deena. Whoever did this planned ahead and broke the lock so they could come after school to steal from Mr. Bennet. It might just be candy that was taken, but the intent is a much bigger crime."

I declared. "I need you to be honest, if you did this, you need to come clean right now, or you are going to be in a whole mess of trouble."

"I didn't do it," she cried.

I was quite certain that she had done this. However, I could usually get her to come around and spit out the truth. She just wasn't giving in. I went for a final push.

"Deena this school has cameras. I'm going to check the recording yesterday to see who went into Mr. Bennet room after school. If I see you on the video...I don't know what will happen, but it won't be good. This is your last chance, to come clean and tell us the truth."

She was silent for nearly 5 minutes. "Fine."

"Fine what?"

"I took the candy."

"Did you jam the lock?"

"Ya. Am I still in trouble? Since I told the truth?"

"I'm afraid so. You had many chances to tell the truth. I can't save you from consequences. I'll ask the principal how he would like us to handle it."

Since this was the fourth time Deena had been caught for stealing, since it took an enormous amount of pressure to get her to tell the truth, since she had gone further with planning ahead and jamming the lock, the police were called. The officer scared her pretty good.

"The next time you steal anything, no matter what it is, you are going to jail and then to court." The officer barked. "You are lucky these teachers aren't pressing charges, or I would be taking you in right now."

Deena spent the entire day with me. She had been busted a total of four times for stealing from teachers, but this time the Police were called and she received a case number. She spent the remainder of the day helping me clean my room. Deena is incredibly smart but it is very difficult to know how to help her. I see great potential in her ability. She does very well in afterschool activities, but she continues to steal, lie, and make bad choices. Her classroom teacher is obviously completely fed up with her. I was very embarrassed, as I always defend her, but am not sure I can continue to do so. Having the officer come really helped.
Deena didn't get in trouble for stealing again, at least for the rest of 5th grade, and she was better at coming clean with the truth when she was caught in a lie. The rest of the school year had a few bumps, but for the most part, Deena did well and showed incredible growth.

My experiences with Deena reveal that it is very difficult for me to not take it personally when the students are not successful. It feels like the program is failing and so am I.
Her classroom teacher is a bit difficult to work with as he doesn't reply to emails and doesn't return paperwork. I was very frustrated when Deena had her first great week and earned teacher time—she was all set to help me teach the second graders, then her classroom teacher took it away because she had lied to him. It was a difficult situation because she had earned it the week prior and the consequence was hard to justify. Collaborating with other teachers could be problematic because we each have a way of doing things.

Lagging Skills	Fall	Spring
1. Difficulty handling transitions, shifting from one mindset or task to another.	2	1
2. Difficulty doing things in a logical sequence or prescribed order.	2	1
3. Difficulty persisting on challenging or tedious tasks.	2	1
4. Poor sense of time.	3	1
5. Difficulty reflecting on multiple thoughts or ideas simultaneously.	2	1
6. Difficulty maintaining focus.	3	1
7. Difficulty considering the likely outcomes or consequences of actions (impulsive).	3	2
8. Difficulty considering a range of solutions to a problem.	2	1
9. Difficulty expressing concerns, needs, or thoughts in words.	1	1
10. Difficulty understanding what is being said.	0	0
11. Difficulty managing emotional response to frustration so as to think rationally.	2	1
12. Chronic irritability and/or anxiety significantly impede capacity for problem-solvi	1	1
13. Difficulty seeing the "grays"/concrete, literal, black-and-white, thinking.	1	1
14. Difficulty deviating from rules, routine.	1	1
15. Difficulty handling unpredictability, ambiguity, uncertainty, novelty.	1	1
16. Difficulty shifting from original idea, plan, or solution.	1	1
17. Difficulty taking into account situational factors that would suggest the need to ad	2	2
18. Inflexible, inaccurate interpretations/cognitive distortions or biases (e.g., "Everyo "Nobody likes me," "You always blame me, "It's not fair," "I'm stupid")	3	1
19. Difficulty attending to or accurately interpreting social cues/poor perception of so	2	1
20. Difficulty starting conversations, entering groups, connecting with people/lacking	3	1
21. Difficulty seeking attention in appropriate ways.	2	1
22. Difficulty appreciating how his/her behavior is affecting other people.	3	2
23. Difficulty empathizing with others, appreciating another person's perspective or p	3	2
24. Difficulty appreciating how s/he is coming across or being perceived by others.	2	2

SCHOOL- Unsolved Problems

	Fall	Spring
1. Shifting from one specific task to another.	3	2
2. Getting started on/completing class assignments.	3	2
3. Interactions with a particular classmate/teacher.	2	1
4. Behavior in hallway/at recess/in cafeteria/on school bus/waiting in line.	1	1
5. Talking at appropriate times.	2	2
6. Academic tasks/demands, e.g., writing assignments.	2	2
7. Handling disappointment/losing at a game/not coming in first/not being first in line	2	1

Figure 9.2 Deena's ALSUP

Anthony

Slumped over, with his head on the table, sat Anthony. His lethargy was almost contagious. I knew Anthony came from a single parent household with six children. I suspected parental neglect, but it was terribly hard to prove it. Maslow's hierarchy of needs came to mind, as I discovered the challenge of working with students who are lacking basic needs.

"Anthony you look really tired today."

"Ya, I am. I was up late watching tv."

"How late do you think you were up?"

"I'm not sure but I watched Family Guy."

"Wow! That show is on at 1am, if you watched the whole show you didn't go to sleep until after 2am! If you get up at 6am that mean you are getting less than 4 hours sleep. Do you stay up late often?"

"Ya. Almost every night."

It was obvious that Anthony was not getting adequate sleep at night. Anthony struggled the most with handling disappointments. He loved to have computer time, but when he lost the privilege or his time was cut short he had an extremely difficult time managing his emotions. He also struggled in his interactions with others, specifically considering solutions. Like most students he lacked academic motivation as well. I often wondered what role an increase in sleep would play in his executive function abilities. After calling home and suffering through a belittling conversation with his mother, I knew my advice for extra sleep would only go as far as my conversations with Anthony. I tried to make it clear to him how important sleep was. Anthony did listen to me, and he acknowledged that he needed more sleep, but when you're 10 years old, there's only so much you can do. He may have agreed, but may not have had the parental guidance to implement it.

Anthony displayed the most improvement of all the students in the intervention program. His ALSUP score decreased 41 points from 67 to 26. His school referrals declined drastically, the previous year he had been written up 38 times, this year only 9. He was a joy to work with and displayed the most eagerness to achieve his goals.

Lagging Skills	Fall	Spring
1. Difficulty handling transitions, shifting from one mindset or task to another.	3	2
2. Difficulty doing things in a logical sequence or prescribed order.	3	1
3. Difficulty persisting on challenging or tedious tasks.	1	1
4. Poor sense of time.	3	1
5. Difficulty reflecting on multiple thoughts or ideas simultaneously.	1	0
6. Difficulty maintaining focus.	3	1
7. Difficulty considering the likely outcomes or consequences of actions (impulsive).	3	1
8. Difficulty considering a range of solutions to a problem.	3	0
9. Difficulty expressing concerns, needs, or thoughts in words.	1	0
10. Difficulty understanding what is being said.	1	0
11. Difficulty managing emotional response to frustration so as to think rationally.	3	2
12. Chronic irritability and/or anxiety significantly impede capacity for problem-solvi	1	1
13. Difficulty seeing the "grays"/concrete, literal, black-and-white, thinking.	3	1
14. Difficulty deviating from rules, routine.	1	0
15. Difficulty handling unpredictability, ambiguity, uncertainty, novelty.	2	0
16. Difficulty shifting from original idea, plan, or solution.	1	0
17. Difficulty taking into account situational factors that would suggest the need to ad	2	0
18. Inflexible, inaccurate interpretations/cognitive distortions or biases (e.g., "Everyo "Nobody likes me," "You always blame me, "It's not fair," "I'm stupid")	2	1
19. Difficulty attending to or accurately interpreting social cues/poor perception of so	1	0
20. Difficulty starting conversations, entering groups, connecting with people/lacking	1	0
21. Difficulty seeking attention in appropriate ways.	3	1
22. Difficulty appreciating how his/her behavior is affecting other people.	2	1
23. Difficulty empathizing with others, appreciating another person's perspective or p	1	0
24. Difficulty appreciating how s/he is coming across or being perceived by others.	1	0

SCHOOL- Unsolved Problems

1. Shifting from one specific task to another.	3	1
2. Getting started on/completing class assignments.	3	2
3. Interactions with a particular classmate/teacher.	3	2
4. Behavior in hallway/at recess/in cafeteria/on school bus/waiting in line.	3	0
5. Talking at appropriate times.	3	2
6. Academic tasks/demands, e.g., writing assignments.	3	2
7. Handling disappointment/losing at a game/not coming in first/not being first in line	3	3

OTHER- Unsolved Problems

Figure 9.3 Anthony's ALSUP

Wade

Wade had the most trouble getting his journal signed, although I reminded him several times. When he had earned no points for those days it seemed to be a good consequence. However, Wade became very angry with me when he did not earn his reward incentive and proceeded to tear his journal apart, page by page, scattering it in a trail across my classroom. It felt as though he was looking for attention, so after asking him to stop I ignored him. When he was done he went back to class. I called his classroom teacher and explained what had happened and asked for him to come back and pick up his journal, which he did.

Wade struggled most of the school year to stay on track with the program. In the spring he was having extreme difficulty. He came to meet with me one day after his classroom teacher had tried every redirection. It was obvious Wade wasn't getting enough sleep at night. His unstable living situation meant he had no bedroom or personal bed to sleep in. He slept on the living room floor. The lack of adult supervision promoted his ability to watch television late into the night.

I asked Wade if I could give him a stress test to determine the level of stress in his life. He agreed and I began asking him questions on the ACEs checklist. When Wade answered "yes" I would prod for further details. "Can you tell me more about that?" He shared with me about his sleeping conditions. "I'm afraid to go to my mom's. She freaks out and starts yelling at me and my little sister. She hits me with a hanger."

I could feel the tear swelling in my eyes as Wade continued his sharing. Soon I couldn't hold back anymore and my warm tears trickled down my cheeks. "Ms. Laabs, why are you crying?" He asked.

"I'm crying for you, because I feel your pain right now. I think this makes sense to me why you are having so much trouble in school. You have very high levels of stress (trauma) at home. All this stress makes it difficult for you to function in school. You have a hard time controlling yourself and then you get in trouble. It's not your fault."

"It's not my fault?"

"No, I don't believe it is."

"I'm not a bad boy?"

"No, Wade, you are not a bad boy. You have an extreme amount of stress going on at home and you have difficulty dealing with it, making learning and following classroom expectations even harder."

"I'm not a bad boy?"

"No. You are a good boy"

"But I keep getting in trouble and everyone thinks I'm bad."

"I don't think you're bad. Look at your stress score its 7 out of 10. Other students might have a 4 or 3. You have a very high level of stress in your life.

"Can you please show this to my teacher? Can you please tell her I'm not bad?"

"Sure, I will talk with her after school"

"No right now, it is important, I need you to tell her right now."

Working with Wade became more and more difficult over the school year. The last two months of school it became very difficult, almost impossible to get him to stay focused on the procedures of the intervention. On the days he was totally out of control I noticed a look in his eyes. A very empty look, as if he was not there and something else had taken over his body.

Lagging Skills	Fall	Spring
1. Difficulty handling transitions, shifting from one mindset or task to another.	1	1
2. Difficulty doing things in a logical sequence or prescribed order.	1	1
3. Difficulty persisting on challenging or tedious tasks.	1	2
4. Poor sense of time.	2	1
5. Difficulty reflecting on multiple thoughts or ideas simultaneously.	1	1
6. Difficulty maintaining focus.	1	2
7. Difficulty considering the likely outcomes or consequences of actions (impulsive).	2	2
8. Difficulty considering a range of solutions to a problem.	1	2
9. Difficulty expressing concerns, needs, or thoughts in words.	2	2
10. Difficulty understanding what is being said.	1	2
11. Difficulty managing emotional response to frustration so as to think rationally.	2	2
12. Chronic irritability and/or anxiety significantly impede capacity for problem-solvi	1	1
13. Difficulty seeing the "grays"/concrete, literal, black-and-white, thinking.	1	1
14. Difficulty deviating from rules, routine.	1	1
15. Difficulty handling unpredictability, ambiguity, uncertainty, novelty.	1	1
16. Difficulty shifting from original idea, plan, or solution.	1	1
17. Difficulty taking into account situational factors that would suggest the need to ad	1	1
18. Inflexible, inaccurate interpretations/cognitive distortions or biases (e.g., "Everyo "Nobody likes me," "You always blame me, "It's not fair," "I'm stupid")	2	2
19. Difficulty attending to or accurately interpreting social cues/poor perception of so	2	1
20. Difficulty starting conversations, entering groups, connecting with people/lacking	1	1
21. Difficulty seeking attention in appropriate ways.	1	1
22. Difficulty appreciating how his/her behavior is affecting other people.	1	1
23. Difficulty empathizing with others, appreciating another person's perspective or p	2	1
24. Difficulty appreciating how s/he is coming across or being perceived by others.	1	1
SCHOOL- Unsolved Problems		
1. Shifting from one specific task to another.	1	1
2. Getting started on/completing class assignments.	1	1
3. Interactions with a particular classmate/teacher.	2	1
4. Behavior in hallway/at recess/in cafeteria/on school bus/waiting in line.	3	3
5. Talking at appropriate times.	1	2
6. Academic tasks/demands, e.g., writing assignments.	2	2
7. Handling disappointment/losing at a game/not coming in first/not being first in line	2	3
OTHER- Unsolved Problems		
1. Organization	2	1

Figure 9.4 Wade's ALSUP

Concluding Thoughts

Together, these stories reveal that executive function skills can indeed be improved through intervention, even though each individual responds differently. Implementing this intervention was both challenging and rewarding for me. Dividing my attention between teaching all my normal classes and administering this behavior program was challenging and stressful. I found that it was difficult to switch gears mentally from one to the other. The behavior students easily called for my time and my attention. I wanted to give them as much of my time as I could which made it very difficult to say no. Soon I was spending my lunchtime, breaks, and each available moment in effort to help these students. It was exhausting. When the students had a difficult day, it was hard for me not to take personal responsibility for it. I guess this is what they call "caretaker fatigue."

If I were to conduct a similar version again I would hope my attention could be fully towards the interventions, and not split between other duties. I would also stress to the classroom teachers the importance of their full support and "buy in" of the program. Consistency is crucial in a program like this, and proves to be beneficial for struggling students. The intervention program seemed to produce the best results when the classroom teacher was the most supportive. If the classroom teacher didn't fully support the program, or was inconsistent with sending the students for check-ins, their success was hindered.

Previously, I had little experience conducting an in-depth behavior intervention program; this was indeed a totally new experience for me. I also had never used SWIS data before. I gained experience and learning in how to use SWIS data effectively. I was able to run analysis on when, where, and what behaviors are occurring. This stretched me in new ways because I needed to analyze the SWIS reports and then comparatively find ways of motivating behaviorally challenged students, and most importantly, developing a way to track their individual progress in a manner which I can effectively communicate the results with others.

This intervention ultimately affected the students, as well as my own development as a teacher. The behavior intervention program directly impacted the students who participated. I feel strongly that this program was helpful and beneficial to the students and the classroom behaviors as a method of interrupting unwanted behaviors in the classroom. The school was delighted to see the program results and would like to offer more intervention programs like it.

For the most part, the intervention was effective. However, there were times when the intervention did not work at all. For example, when a student might slip and have a bad day early in the week and then they would either brag that they didn't care about whatever the reward activity was, or they would throw a fit and have an awful week if they knew early on they had blown their chances of earning a reward. Keeping the reward a secret seemed to work much better for these students. Friday reward activities would be computer time, building or making something, doing nails for girls, ice cream sundaes, etc. My favorite reward was making catapults and shooting mini-marshmallows at each other.

Students who have experienced high level of ACEs tend to demonstrate a deficit in executive function and self-regulation, and as a result they exhibit explosive behaviors in the classroom. As teachers we must work within the realm of the school day, since we cannot control what traumas the students may face at home. However, we can promote executive function and self-regulation in the classroom through interventions that focus on addressing student needs through not continuing a cycle of trauma but rather giving metacognitive support and coping power to students.

Chapter 10: Conclusion

In the beginning of this book, I laid out several research questions. I have endeavored to answer these questions through demonstrating my own life in memoir. The beauty of autoethnography is the self-reflexive nature through which the researcher engages with the research. This process of inquiry has produced for me the opportunity to make sense of my own experience, while also reaching out to others. Through provoking my own deep and troubling emotions, I have resolved to seek not only understanding, but the opportunity to provide some answers and help to others.

This project has, in essence, been developing for my entire life. Most people who implement behavior interventions are unlikely to have experienced high levels of trauma, if any at all. This leads to the power behind this autoethnographic piece. I examine trauma, executive function and resilience, and apply it directly to an educational setting *with the awareness of my own experience*. Being a reflexive subject permits me to interweave my role as a researcher and participant. However, this approach does not have to end with me and my personal gains. The method of writing autoethnographically leads to the natural invitation of readers to be a part of the study—to reflect, to absorb, and to take away a better understanding of situations that they may not have experienced themselves, but their students may not be able to fully express. At the very least, I hope educators can become aware of how important it is to evaluate more than a student's work.

In the classroom, it seems that students are exhibiting difficulty more and more prominently. As educators, we are charged with assessing students' academic abilities, but why not executive functional abilities? It seems as though these are closely connected. What if traditional education moved into a paradigm shift of encompassing therapeutic development alongside academics? How might the achievement gap be affected if students were educated on strengthening their reading and writing skills, but also their self-regulation skills? As an educator I have very little influence on what happens in a student's life beyond my classroom. However, I can look critically at the bigger picture in the student's life. I want to know what is going on at home, and what a child has experienced because it will help me understand why a child might be acting the way they are.

For those educators moved by this piece, there are some resources. Of course, they can adapt the methods that I implemented in my behavior intervention described in chapter nine. Additionally, Knight (2007) developed a three-dimensional resilience framework (emotional competence, social competence and futures-oriented) as a universal tool to explore and describe the concept of resilience for educators. Knight (2007) explained emotional competence as the ability to have an internal locus of control, sense of humor and positive self-esteem. Having social competence meant that a student would have the ability to engage in healthy communication, benefit from supportive relationships and was able to have empathy towards others. Knight (2007, p. 548) suggested that a student who is futures-oriented was able to have a "clear sense of purpose and feeling that one's life has meaning; sense of optimism; being able to engage in problem solving and critical reflection; and have the ability to be flexible and adaptive in new situations."

I hope this book provides insight for other educators in understanding, relating, and implementing interventions to help students who may be exhibiting executive function difficulty. I urge them to take the next steps.

Future Research

While my experience here offers a glimpse, further investigation is needed to thoroughly understand the connections between executive function and resilience. Can interventions indeed "rewire" the brain's executive function? This study can be treated as exploratory, opening the way for further research.

Based on my findings here and experiences in the classroom, I also recommend and intend to pursue further research into the role of boundaries and how children process them in relation to resilience. In chapter eight, I briefly touch upon this subject in relation to my own resilience. Yet, further work is needed. As children learn how to set and uphold boundaries, how do they react when bending the rules is permitted? For instance, hitting is never ok. But we allow boxing, and we celebrate the actions of the winner. While this is an extreme example, our complex societies produce a massive grey area between the rigid lines we draw. How do children process these boundaries, and how do they relate to executive function?

I also encourage research on the relationship between animal therapy and resilience, which I also briefly mention in chapter eight. I firmly believe the interaction between humans and animals helps with resilience, specifically in the classroom. I have begun to investigate this relationship through adding a rabbit to my classroom. The rabbit is litter trained and is at times allowed to hop around the classroom. The interaction between the students and this animal has been phenomenal. Students who previously exhibited explosive behaviors, now are better able to self-regulate as they desire to complete their work to spend time with the animal. Researchers in this field must now ask: What is the connection between self-regulation and the presence of animals? After all, the animals in my classroom require students to be calm, and gentle, and control impulses.

Intervention efforts may also benefit from an analysis of multiple areas of competency. Not only does this serve to provide the individual with identified areas of strength, but it also fosters awareness of potential vulnerabilities. As discussed in this study, overall mental health may be potentially vulnerable to life stress. Future directions in terms of this investigation could include design modifications to identify specific aspects of the processes associated with resilience. Assessing both the kind of stressful events and symptoms with greater specificity may prove informative.

Beyond this one, few studies have assessed interventions geared specifically towards improving executive function as protective moderators within the construct of resilience. The results of the behavior interventions identify that both executive functions and social skills development serve as decreasing classroom behavior infractions, although perhaps not uniformly or always in the expected direction. The utility of this executive function strengthening as behavioral intervention sources, if taken with an awareness of ACES's does indeed provide capacity to foster positive adaptation in the context of high-risk.

Final Reflections

This study reflects the larger path of my development from a "bad kid" to a teacher. Through slowly learning the mega-cognitive skills of executive function, I have come to a point wherein I can self-reflexively look back at my life of adversity and resilience, up to this point, and create something positive from it.

Through my education and career, I learned to create boundaries, to trust again, and to verbalize my frustration by expressing my feelings instead of deferring to the use of verbal banter. I have found this process to be both therapeutic and enlightening. As I have strived toward healing, understanding and a healthier life the relationships with my immediate family have also become stronger. The steps taken toward becoming resilient, though sometimes small, were necessary in order to move to living an improved life. Moreover, the significance of taking steps did not warrant self-pity, but focused on my new-found independence.

This empowerment has allowed me to impact students and family members alike who have sought ways out of poverty and abuse. Once I found that I had a purpose and my life had meaning, I became optimistic about what life had to offer. Even the bumps on the way to attaining my professional career and educational goals allowed me to problem solve and reflect critically on the steps I needed to take next. At times, it required that I be more flexible or encourage me to be more adaptive to a new scenario. I was future-oriented.

I challenge you, as I constantly challenge myself, to stop blaming the individual and seek ways to improve.

References

Borbasi, S. (1994). Insider Ethnography. *Nursing Inquiry (1)*, 57.

Bronfenbrenner. (1979). Ecology of Human Development.

Burke, N. J., Hellman, J. L., Scott, B. G., Weems, C. F., & Carrion, V. G. (2011). The Impact of Adverse Childhood Experiences On An Urban Pediatric Population. *Child Abuse & Neglect*, Vol.35(6), pp.408-413.

Burns, J. (2005). *Preliminary Report- Grant 790: Alternative Education Program.* Malden, MA: Department of Education.

Edleson, J. (1999). The Overlap Between Child Maltreatment and Women Battering. *Violence Against Women*, 5(2): 134-154.

Ellis, C., & Bochner, A. (2000). Autoethnography, Personal Narrative, Reflexivity: Researcher as Subject. In N. a. Denzin, *The Handbook of Qualitative Research* (pp. 733-768). Newbury Park, CA: Sage.

Elvove, E., Tedeschi, P., & Brandes, H. (Eds.). (2015). Growing Together: Children, Animals and Sowing the Seeds of Resiliency. *Green Chimneys Human-Animal Interaction Conference Summary.* Brewster, New York, USA: University of Denver Graduate School of Social Work.

Erwin, J. (2004). *The Classroom of Choice: Giving Students What They Need and Getting What You Want.* Alexandria, VA: Association for Supervision and Curriculm Development.

Felitti, V. J., Anda, R. F., Nordenberg, D., Williamson, D. F., Spitz, A. M., Edwards, V, J. S. (1998). Relationship of Childhood Abuse and Household Dysfunction to Many of the Leading Causes of Death in Adults The Adverse Childhood Experiences (ACE) Study. *American Journal of Preventive Medicine, Vol. 14 (4)*, 245-258.

Greenberg, M. T. (2006). Promoting Resilience in Children and Youth. *Annals New Yorj Academy of Sciences*, 139-150.

Greene, R. (2008). Kids Do Well If They Can. *Phi Delta Kappan*, 160-167.

Herman, J. (1997). *Trauma and Recovery.* New York, NY: Basic Books.

Janoff-Bulman, R. (1992). *Shattered Assumptions: Towards a New Psychology of Trauma.* New York, NY: Free Press.

Knight, C. (2007). A resilience framework: perspectives for educators,. *Health Education, 107*, 543 – 555.

Lewis, D. M. (1989). Child Abuse, Juvenile Deliquency, and Violent Criminality. In D. a. Chicchetti (Ed.), *Child Maltreatment* (pp. 707-721). Cambridge: Cambridge University Press.

Lochman, J. E., Wells, K. C., & Lenhart, L. A. (2006). *Coping Power Program.* Oxford: Oxford University Press. Retrieved from Coping Power: http://www.copingpower.com/

Massachusetts Advocates for Children. (2005). *Healping Traumatized Children Learn.* Boston, MA: Harvard Law School.

Masten, A. S. (2012). Executive Function Skills and School Success in Young Children Experiencing Homelessness. *Educational Researcher, Vol. 41*, 375-384.

Masten, A. S. (2014). *Ordinary Magic: Resilience in Development.* New York, NY: The Guilford Press.

McCloskey, G. P. (2009). *Assessment and Intervention of Executive Function Difficulties.* New York, NY: Routledge.

McCloskey, G., Perkins, L. A., & Van Divner, B. (2009). *Assessment and Intervention of Executive Function Difficulties.* New York, NY: Routledge.

McEwen, B. (2004). Protection and Damage from Acute and Chronic Stress: Allostasis and Allostatic Overload and Relevance to the Pathophysiology of Psychiatric Disorders. *Annals of the New York Academy of Sciences*, 1032: 1–7.

McEwen, B. (2006). Protective and Damaging Effects of Stress Mediators: Central Role of the Brain. *Dialogues Clin Neurosci*, 367-381.

Mead, G. (1934). *Mind, Self and Society*. Chicago, IL: University of Chicago Press.

Muncey, T. (2010). *Creating Autoethnographies*. Thousand Oaks, CA: SAGE Publications Inc. .

Patton, M. Q. (2002). *Qualitative Research & Evaluation Methods (3rd ed.)*. Thousand Oaks CA: Sage.

Pittman, K. I. (2000). *Unfinished business: Further reflections on a decade of promoting youth development*. Takoma Park, MD: The Forum for Youth Investment.

Reda, M. M. (2007, March 22). *Autoethnography as research methodology?* Retrieved from The Free Library: http://www.thefreelibrary.com/Autoethnography as research methodology?-a0165912665

Reed-Danahay, D. E. (1997). *Auto/Ethnography: Rewriting the self and the social*. Oxford, NY: Berg.

Ritter, J., Stewart, M., Bernet, C., & Coe, M. (2002). Effects of Chilhood Exposure to Familial Alcoholism and Family Violence on Adolescent Substance Abuse, Conduct Problems, and Self-Esteem. *Journal of Traumatic Stress*, 15(2): 113-122.

Sapolsky, R. M. (1994). *Why Zebras Don't get Ulcers*. New York, NY: St. Martin's Press.

Shonkoff, J. &. (2012). The Lifelong Effects of Early Childhood Adversity and Toxic Stress. *American Academy of Pediatrics, Vol. 129.*, 232-246.

Shonkoff, J., Garner, A., & The Committee on Psychosocial Aspects of the Child and Family Health, C. o. (2012). The Lifelong Effects of Early Childhood Adversity and Toxic Stress. *American Academy of Pediatrics*, 232-246.

Spinazzola, J., Ford, J., Zucker, M., van der Kolk, B., Silva, S., Smith, S., & Blaustein, M. (2005). Survey Evaluates Complex Trauma Exposure, Outcome, and Intervention Amoung Children and Adolescents. *Psychiatric Annals*, 35 (5): 433-439.

Spry, T. (2001). Performing autoethnography: An embodies methodological praxis. *Qualitative Inquiry*, 706-732.

Sroufe, A. (1997). Psychopathology as an Outcome Development. *Development and Psychopathology*, 9:251-268; 262.

Terr, L. (1991). Childhood Traumas: An Outline and Overview. *American Journal of Psychiatry*, 148: 10-20.

Tough, P. (2012). *How Children Succeed.* New York, NY: Houghton Mifflin Harcourt.

Toxic Stress. (2015, 11 17). Retrieved from Center on the Developing Child Harvard University: http://developingchild.harvard.edu/science/key-concepts/toxic-stress/

Van der Kolk, B. (2005). Developmental Trauma Disorder. *Psychriatric Annals*, 35: 401-408.

Wolcott, H. (2001). *Writing Up Qualitative Research (2nd edn).* Thousand Oaks, CA: SAGE.

Wolin, S., & Wolin, S. (1993). *The resilient self: how survivors of troubled families rise above adversity.* New York: Villiard.